Windows® 10
PORTABLE GENIUS

Paul McFedries

WILEY

About the Author

Paul McFedries is a technical writer who has been authoring computer books since 1991 and has nearly 100 books to his credit. Paul's books have sold more than four million copies worldwide. These books include the Wiley titles *Teach Yourself VISUALLY Windows 10,*Third Edition, *G Suite For Dummies, iPhone Portable Genius,* Sixth Edition, and *iPad Portable Genius,* Fourth Edition. You can visit Paul on the web at www.mcfedries.com or on Twitter at www.twitter.com/paulmcf.

Acknowledgments

The only thing more fun than using Windows is writing a book about it! That's particularly true for an interesting project such as this book, which was made all the more pleasant by the great people I got to work with. They include Associate Publisher Jim Minatel, who was kind enough to ask me to write the book; Project Editor Kezia Endsley, whose just-so suggestions and penetrating questions made this a better book; Copy Editor Kim Cofer, whose eagle-eye for all things ungrammatical made me look like a better writer than I am; and Technical Editor Vince Averello, whose knowledge of the Windows world is nothing short of amazing. Many thanks to all of you for outstanding work on this project.

Contents

Acknowledgments   iii

Introduction   x

chapter 1

How Do I Customize Windows?   2

Working with Settings   4
     Opening the Settings app   4
     Synchronizing settings
     between PCs   6
     Accessing an app's settings   6
Customizing the Start Menu   7
     Pinning an app to the Start menu   7
     Arranging and sizing Start
     menu tiles   8
     Customizing Start menu settings   9
Customizing the Taskbar   10
     Pinning an app to the taskbar   10
     Customizing taskbar settings   11
     Customizing the taskbar's
     notification area   13
Customizing the Lock Screen   15
     Changing the Lock screen
     background   16
     Adding an app to the Lock screen   17
Extending Your Desktop with
Multiple Monitors   18

Setting Up Multiple Desktops   20
     Adding a new desktop   20
     Switching to another desktop   21
     Moving an app to a different
     desktop   22

chapter 2

How Can I Make the Most of Surfing the Web?   24

Taking Advantage of Tabs   26
     Opening a link in a new tab   26
     Creating a new tab   26
     Customizing the new tab page   26
     Navigating tabs   28
     Duplicating a tab   28
     Pinning a tab   28
     Controlling which tabs
     appear at startup   28
     Closing tabs   30
Saving Your Favorite Pages   30
     Adding a page to the
     Favorites list   30
     Working with the Favorites
     bar   31
     Opening a page from the
     Favorites list   33
     Maintaining favorites   33

Customizing Edge   34
  Changing the Edge search
  engine   34
  Changing the theme   35
  Setting the default zoom level   36
  Customizing the toolbar   37
  Customizing the font   39

chapter 3

How Do I Maximize Sending and Receiving Email? 42

Managing Mail Accounts   44
  Adding an account   44
  Changing the account name   46
  Deleting an account   47
Setting Options for Incoming
Messages   47
  Customizing account sync
  settings   48
  Combining the Focused
  and Other tabs   49
  Grouping messages individually   49
  Controlling notifications   50
  Switching between accounts   51
Setting Send Options   51
  Creating a signature   51
  Setting the default message font   52
  Changing your message priority   54
  Running the spell-checker to
  eliminate message errors   55

chapter 4

Can I Use Windows to Manage Contacts and Appointments? 58

Managing Your Contacts   60
  Adding contacts from
  an existing account   60
  Creating a contact   62
  Viewing contacts   64
  Editing a contact   65
  Assigning a photo to a contact   65

  Creating a new contact
  from an electronic business card   67
  Filtering your contacts   68
  Linking multiple profiles
  to a contact   69
  Deleting a contact   70
Tracking Your Events   71
  Viewing your calendar   71
  Adding an event to your
  calendar   72
  Creating a recurring event   73
  Adding an event reminder   74
  Setting up an online meeting   74
  Customizing your calendar   76

chapter 5

What Other Day-to-Day Tasks Can I Perform? 78

Finding Stuff on Your PC   80
  Viewing your timeline   80
  Searching your PC   80
Configuring the Cortana
Voice Assistant   83
  Controlling your PC
  with Cortana   84
Making Video Calls   85
  Configuring Skype   85
  Calling someone using
  Skype   86
  Dealing with an incoming
  Skype call   86
Working with Maps   87
  Giving Maps access to
  your location   87
  Displaying a location
  on a map   88
  Getting directions
  to a location   90
Checking the Weather   93
  Checking your weather
  forecast   93
  Checking another city's
  weather forecast   95

chapter 6

How Do I Max Out the Windows Image Tools?   96

Getting Images into Your PC   98
Importing images from a smartphone
or digital camera   98
Scanning an image   99
Taking a picture or video with your PC camera   101
Viewing Your Images   103
Using File Explorer to view your images   103
Using the Photos app to view your images   104
Starting a slide show   106
Enhancing Your Images   107
Cropping an image   107
Applying a filter   108
Adding a vignette effect   110
Repairing Your Images   111
Rotating an image   111
Straightening an image   111
Adjusting the light   112
Adjusting the colors   114
Enhancing image clarity   115
Getting rid of red eye   115
Fixing small flaws   116

chapter 7

Can I Share My Computer?   118

Sharing Your PC via User Accounts   120
Creating a user account   120
Switching between accounts   122
Changing your user account picture   125
Changing the account type   126
Deleting an account   127

Sharing Your PC with a Child   127
Adding a child to your PC   128
Setting restrictions on a child's account   128
Sharing PC Resources   132
Sharing a document or folder   132
Switching to advanced sharing   134
Sharing a folder with other users on the network   135
Protect your shared folders with advanced file permissions   136

chapter 8

How Can I Get More from a Tablet PC?   138

Working in Tablet Mode   140
Controlling Windows with Gestures   141
Understanding gestures   142
Using gestures to control Windows   142
Inputting Text with the Touch Keyboard   143
Displaying the touch keyboard   143
Selecting a touch keyboard type   144
Using the touch keyboard   145
Entering text using the handwriting panel   147
Configuring the touch keyboard   149
Setting Power and Battery Options   149
Monitoring battery life   150
Setting the power mode   150
Adjusting screen brightness   151
Switching to Battery Saver mode   151
Creating a custom power plan to improve battery life   152
Checking out more ways to save energy   153

vi

chapter 9

How Do I Work with
Documents?   156

Editing Documents   158
  Creating a new document   158
  Saving a document   158
  Opening a document   159
  Changing the text font   160
  Finding text   162
  Replacing text   164
  Inserting special symbols   165
  Saving a copy of a document   167
Taking Notes with OneNote   168
  Creating a OneNote notebook   168
  Adding pages and sections
  to a notebook   168
  Adding and working with
  text notes   170
  Adding an image to a
  notebook page   172
  Working with notebook lists   173
Working with Files   175
  Selecting a file   175
  Changing the file view   176
  Previewing a file   176
  Copying a file   178
  Moving a file   178
  Renaming a document   179
  Creating a new file   180
  Deleting a document   181
  Extracting files from a
  compressed folder   183
  Specifying a different app when
  opening a document   185

chapter 10

What Are Some Ways to
Enhance PC Security?   188

Enhancing Sign-In Security   190
  Creating a strong password   190
  Updating your account
  password   191

  Creating a picture password   192
  Signing in with a PIN   193
  Setting up a fingerprint sign-in   194
Locking Your PC to Prevent
Others from Using It   195
  Locking your computer   196
  Configuring your PC to lock
  automatically   196
Enhancing Your Privacy   198
  Making the Start menu more
  private   198
  Controlling your private
  information   199
  Stopping an app's notifications   201
  Clearing your activity history   201
  Resetting your computer
  to preserve privacy   202

chapter 11

How Do I Increase Internet
Privacy and Security?   204

Making the Web More Secure   206
  Avoiding viruses   206
  Opting to never save a site's
  password   208
  Deleting a saved website
  password   208
Making the Web More Private   209
  Deleting your browsing data to
  ensure privacy   209
  Turning on private browsing   211
  Preventing ad sites from
  tracking you online   211
  Enabling strict tracking
  prevention   212
  Preventing sites from
  requesting your location   213
Enhancing Email Security and
Privacy   215
  Avoiding viruses in email   215
  Preventing messages from
  opening automatically   216
  Thwarting web bugs by
  blocking images in messages   216
  Avoiding phishing scams   217

chapter 12

How Do I Maintain Windows?   220

Performing a Few Maintenance
Chores   222
    Scheduling automatic
    maintenance   222
    Checking hard drive free space 223
    Deleting unnecessary files   225
Safeguarding Your Files   226
    Keeping a history of your files 226
    Restoring a file from your
    history   227
    Creating a system image
    backup   228

Using the Windows Recovery
Environment   229
    Understanding the Recovery
    Environment's tools   229
    Accessing the Recovery
    Environment   230
Working with a Recovery Drive   233
    Creating the recovery drive 233
    Booting your PC using
    the recovery drive   234
Working with Restore Points   235
    Creating a system restore point 235
    Reverting to an earlier
    restore point   235

Index   238

Introduction

If you head down to your local bookstore (assuming, of course, that by the time you read this, the entities known as "local bookstores" still exist) and peruse the Computer Books section, you'll almost certainly see several Windows books that are nothing less than gargantuan. We're talking here about books that weigh in at well over a thousand pages and make even the thickest phone book (again, assuming such a thing exists in your time) look like a mere pamphlet.

Who would want to read such a book, much less *write* one? Well, as someone who has written more than one of them, I can tell you the answer with some authority: Windows is a sprawling, complex beast that some say is easily the most complicated piece of software ever created. If you want to teach people everything there is to know about Windows, then the resulting tome is going to be big—*very* big.

Ah, but there's the rub: How many people want or even *need* to learn everything there is to know about Windows? That's right: very few. The rest of us just want to know how to get things done using Windows with a minimum of fuss and as little bother as possible. The rest of us aren't members of the Windows Fan Club; we're not Windows geeks; we don't want to look under the hood to see what makes Windows run. The rest of us have a job to do—a job that means using a Windows PC—and we just want Windows to help as much as it can and then get out of our way. The rest of us, in short, don't need a massive, encyclopedic guide to all things Windows. What we Windows users really need is a reference that's easier to read, more convenient, and doesn't require a regular weight-training regimen to lift. What we really need is a *portable* reference that enables us to be more productive and solve problems wherever we and our PCs happen to be.

Welcome, therefore, to *Windows 10 Portable Genius*. This book is a Windows guide that's presented in an easy-to-use, easy-to-access, and eminently portable format. In this book, you learn how to get more out of Windows by learning how to access all the really powerful and timesaving features that aren't obvious at a casual glance. In this book, you learn how to avoid the more annoying character traits of Windows and, in those cases where such behaviors can't be avoided, you learn how to work around them. In this book, you learn how to prevent Windows problems from occurring, and just in case your preventative measures are for naught, you learn how to fix many common problems yourself.

A few special elements provide guardrails and inspiration. Notes help you delve a bit deeper into some topics, Cautions give advice and help you steer clear of problems, and Genius boxes convey the pro tips that will make you more efficient, more productive, and more impressive in the results that you crank out from Windows.

This book is for Windows users who know the basics but want to take their Windows education to a higher level. It's a book for people who want to be more productive, more efficient, more creative, and more self-sufficient (at least as far as their Windows life goes, anyway). It's a book for people who use Windows every day but want to incorporate Windows into more of their day-to-day activities. It's a book for people who pooh-pooh the notion that you have to be a geek, a nerd, or a computer scientist to get the most out of Windows. It's a book I had a blast writing, so I think it's a book you'll enjoy reading.

How Do I Customize Windows?

← Settings   — □ ×

Windows Settings

Find a setting   🔍

🖥️ **System**
Display, sound, notifications, power

🖫 **Devices**
Bluetooth, printers, mouse

📱 **Phone**
Link your Android, iPhone

🌐 **Network & Internet**
Wi-Fi, airplane mode, VPN

🖌️ **Personalization**
Background, lock screen, colors

▤ **Apps**
Uninstall, defaults, optional features

👤 **Accounts**
Your accounts, email, sync, work, family

🈂️ **Time & Language**
Speech, region, date

🎮 **Gaming**
Xbox Game Bar, captures, Game Mode

♿ **Ease of Access**
Narrator, magnifier, high contrast

🔍 **Search**
Find my files, permissions

🔒 **Privacy**
Location, camera, microphone

🔄 **Update & Security**
Windows Update, recovery, backup

You've probably found that Windows works pretty well right out of the box. Microsoft has configured Windows with default settings that make Windows relatively easy and efficient for most users. Ah, but your purchase of this book shows that you don't fall into the Most Users category. You are your own, unique self, and that uniqueness cries out for and deserves a correspondingly unique Windows experience. Fortunately, as you learn in this chapter, Windows is bristling with tools that enable you to customize almost every aspect of the system, including the Start menu, taskbar, and Lock screen.

Working with Settings...4

Customizing the Start Menu 7

Customizing the Taskbar 10

Customizing the Lock Screen 15

Extending Your Desktop with Multiple Monitors...............18

Setting Up Multiple Desktops.................................20

Working with Settings

Most of your Windows customization work involves tweaking *settings*, which are options—usually in the form of a check box, switch, radio button, or list—that control the look and operation of either Windows itself or of a particular app that's installed on your PC.

Opening the Settings app

When you want to customize Windows, you'll almost always need to open the aptly named Settings app, which is home to most Windows customization options. The Settings app is so important that Windows gives you a dozen or so ways to open it. Here are the six most useful methods:

- Click Start and then click Settings (the gear icon).

- Press Windows+I. (The Windows key is the one that has the Windows logo on it; you'll find it on the lowest row of the keyboard, to the left of the spacebar, between the Ctrl and Alt keys.)

- Click the Notifications icon on the far right of the taskbar and then click All Settings.

- In the taskbar's Search box, type **se** (which should be enough to display the Settings app in the search results; if not, continue typing **settings** until you see Settings in the results) and then press Enter.

- If you have Cortana enabled (see Chapter 5), say "Hey Cortana" and then say "Open Settings."

- Right-click the Start icon and then click Settings.

Whichever method you use, you see the Home screen of the Settings app, as shown in Figure 1.1.

From here, you can either use the Settings app's Search box to locate the setting you want or click a category to see the subcategories and settings associated with that category. For example, Figure 1.2 shows the screen that appears when you click the System category. When you click a subcategory on the left, the settings for that subcategory appear on the right (such as for the Display subcategory shown in Figure 1.2). To return to the previous Settings screen, click the Back arrow in the top-left corner; to return directly to the Home screen, click Home.

1.1 The Home screen of the Settings app.

1.2 When you open a category, click a subcategory on the left to see its settings on the right.

Genius

Use the taskbar's Search box to quickly search for the setting you want to work with. Click inside the taskbar's Search box, type **settings:**, a space, and then begin typing the setting name. For example, to work with the Show More Tiles on Start setting, type **settings: show more**, then click Show More Tiles on Start from the search results that appear.

Synchronizing settings between PCs

If you use the same Microsoft account to sign in to Windows on multiple devices, you can get a more consistent and more efficient experience by synchronizing your settings on all those devices. Here's how to set this up:

1. **Open the Settings app.**

2. **Click Accounts.**

3. **Click Sync Your Settings.** The Sync Your Settings screen appears.

4. **Make sure the Sync Settings switch is set to On.** Click it to toggle it On if needed.

5. **In the Individual Sync Settings section, set the switch to On for each type of setting you want synced.** The four setting types are Theme, Passwords, Language Preferences, and Other Windows Settings.

Accessing an app's settings

Most apps also come with a collection of their own settings, which you can work with to get more out of the app or to customize the app to suit the way you work. For most Windows apps, there are two main ways to access settings:

● Open the app and click Settings (the gear icon), which usually appears in the lower-left corner of the screen (see Figure 1.3).

● In the Start menu, right-click the app, click More, and then click App Settings.

Settings

1.3 For many Windows apps, click Settings (the gear icon) to access the app's options.

Customizing the Start Menu

Although you can use keyboard shortcuts and features such as the taskbar to launch and work with apps and other features, to perform most of your Windows work, you need to negotiate the Start menu. Therefore, you can make your Windows chores easier and more efficient if you take a few moments to customize the Start menu to suit your needs.

Pinning an app to the Start menu

If you have an app that doesn't appear as a tile on the Start menu, you usually open the app by first navigating the Start menu's apps list to locate the app, possibly negotiating one or more submenus along the way. For an app you use often, you can avoid this extra work by *pinning* the app so that it appears permanently on the right side of the Start menu. After you have pinned an app, you launch it by displaying the Start menu and clicking the app.

Follow these steps to pin an app to the Start menu:

1. **Click Start.**

2. **Locate the app that you want to pin to the Start menu.**

3. **Right-click the app and then click Pin to Start.** A tile for the pinned app appears on the right side of the Start menu.

Note To remove an app tile from the Start menu, click Start, right-click the tile, and then click Unpin from Start.

Arranging and sizing Start menu tiles

Here are some useful techniques for restructuring the Start menu's tiles to suit the way you work or play:

- **Move an app tile within the Start menu.** Click Start, then click and drag the app tile to its new position.

- **Group app tiles.** Move an app tile below any existing tile to create a new group. Hover the mouse pointer just above the moved app, then click the Name Group text box that appears. Type your group name (see Figure 1.4) and then press Enter. Move other apps into the new group as needed.

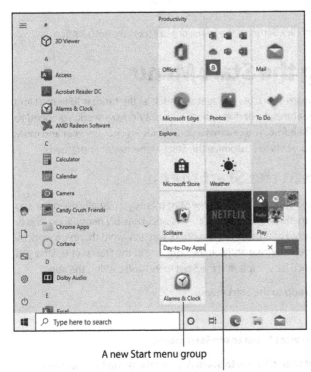

A new Start menu group

Type the group name here

1.4 You can create groups to organize your Start menu apps.

● **Change the size of a Start menu tile.** Click Start, right-click the app's tile, click Resize, and then click the size you want. In all cases, you can choose either a Small or Medium square. With some apps, you can also choose either a Wide rectangle or a Large square.

Customizing Start menu settings

The Start menu offers a few settings that you can tweak to customize how the Start menu works. Open the Settings app, click Personalization, and then click Start. This opens the Start screen (see Figure 1.5), which offers the following switches:

● **Show more tiles on Start.** Set this switch to On to expand the size of the Start menu to show more tiles.

Genius
You can also widen the Start menu by dragging the right edge of the menu.

● **Show app list in Start menu.** Set this switch to Off to remove the list of installed apps from the Start menu. If you set this switch to Off, you can still access the apps by opening the Start menu and then clicking All Apps.

● **Show recently added apps.** Set this switch to On to see newly installed apps at the top of the Start menu's app list.

● **Show most used apps.** Set this switch to On to add a Most Used section to the top of the Start menu's app list. Windows uses the Most Used section to display the apps you launched most frequently.

● **Show suggestions occasionally on Start.** Set this switch to Off to prevent Windows from displaying suggestions (that is, ads) about which apps to install.

● **Use Start full screen.** Set this switch to On to have the Start menu take up the entire screen when you open it.

● **Show recently opened items in Jump Lists on Start or the taskbar and in File Explorer Quick Access.** Set this switch to On to see a Recent section when you right-click an app that enables you to open items such as documents.

● **Choose which folders appear on Start.** Click this link to open the Choose Which Folders Appear on Start screen, which includes a switch for each potential Start menu folder. For each switch, set the switch to On to display the folder, or Off to hide the folder.

Settings   — □ ✕

⌂ Home

| Find a setting   🔎 |

Personalization

🖼 Background

🎨 Colors

🖵 Lock screen

🎨 Themes

🅰 Fonts

🔲 Start

🖵 Taskbar

Start

Show more tiles on Start

⬤⃝ Off

Show app list in Start menu

⬤⬤ On

Show recently added apps

⬤⬤ On

Show most used apps

⬤⃝ Off

Show suggestions occasionally in Start

⬤⬤ On

Use Start full screen

⬤⃝ Off

Show recently opened items in Jump Lists on Start or the taskbar and in File Explorer Quick Access

⬤⬤ On

Choose which folders appear on Start

1.5 Use the Start screen settings to personalize your Start menu.

Customizing the Taskbar

The taskbar that runs across the bottom of the Windows screen gives you one-click access to the Start button, the Search box, the Cortana voice assistant, and Task View (see Chapter 5). The taskbar also enables you to switch to a running app (by clicking the app's taskbar button), access an app's recent documents (by right-clicking the app's button), and launch an app (by clicking its button; see the next section). In short, the taskbar is one of the most useful and most important features in Windows, so you need to know how to customize it to suit your needs. The next few sections tell you everything you need to know.

Pinning an app to the taskbar

Pinning an app to the Start menu, as I discuss earlier in this chapter, is helpful because it puts the app just two clicks away. If you have an app that you use frequently, you might prefer to have that app just a single click away. You can achieve this by pinning the app to the taskbar. You can pin an app to the taskbar either from the Start menu or from the taskbar itself:

- **Pinning an app via the Start menu.** Open the Start menu, right-click the app that you want to pin to the taskbar, click More, and then click Pin to Taskbar.

● **Pinning an app via the Taskbar.** Launch the app that you want to pin to the taskbar, right-click the running app's taskbar icon, and then click Pin to Taskbar.

Either way, Windows adds an icon for the app to the taskbar.

Genius

To change the order of the taskbar icons, drag a taskbar icon to the left or right and then drop it in the new position. Note that this technique applies not only to the icons pinned to the taskbar, but also to the icons for any running programs.

Note

If you no longer want an app pinned to the taskbar, you should remove it to reduce taskbar clutter and provide more room for other app icons. To remove a pinned app icon, right-click the icon and then click Unpin from Taskbar.

Customizing taskbar settings

The taskbar comes with a few settings that enable you to customize the look and operation of the taskbar, which can help you be more productive. Open the Settings app, click Personalization, and then click Taskbar. This opens the Taskbar screen, shown in Figure 1.6.

There are a ton of settings here, so here's a look at the most important ones:

● **Lock the taskbar.** When this switch is On, you can't resize or move the taskbar, and you can't resize or move any taskbar toolbars. This is useful if you share your computer with other users and you don't want to waste time resetting the taskbar if someone else changes it.

Genius

You can also toggle taskbar locking on and off by right-clicking an empty section of the taskbar and then clicking Lock the Taskbar.

● **Automatically hide the taskbar in desktop mode.** When this switch is On, Windows reduces the taskbar to a thin line at the bottom of the screen when you're not using it. This is useful if you want a bit more screen room for your applications. To redisplay the taskbar, move the mouse pointer to the bottom of the screen. Note, however, that you should consider leaving this option unchecked if you use the taskbar frequently; otherwise, auto-hiding it will slow you down because it takes Windows a second or two to restore the taskbar when you hover the mouse pointer over it.

Settings

Home

Find a setting

Personalization

Background

Colors

Lock screen

Themes

Fonts

Start

Taskbar

Taskbar

Lock the taskbar
On

Automatically hide the taskbar in desktop mode
On

Automatically hide the taskbar in tablet mode
On

Use small taskbar buttons
Off

Use Peek to preview the desktop when you move your mouse to the
Show desktop button at the end of the taskbar
On

Replace Command Prompt with Windows PowerShell in the menu
when I right-click the start button or press Windows key+X
On

Show badges on taskbar buttons
On

Taskbar location on screen
Bottom

Combine taskbar buttons
Always, hide labels

1.6 Use the Taskbar screen to customize your taskbar.

- **Automatically hide the taskbar in tablet mode.** This is the same as the preceding switch, except it controls whether the taskbar is hidden when you use tablet mode. (To learn more about tablet mode, see Chapter 8.)

- **Use small taskbar buttons.** Set this switch to On to shrink the taskbar's program buttons. This not only reduces the overall height of the taskbar (so you get more room for the desktop and your programs), but it also enables you to populate the taskbar with more buttons.

- **Use Peek to preview the desktop. . .** Set this switch to On to enable the Peek feature. When you have Peek activated, move the mouse pointer over the right edge of the taskbar, and Windows temporarily hides your open windows so that you can see the desktop. Move the mouse pointer off the right edge of the taskbar to restore your windows.

- **Show badges on taskbar buttons.** Set this switch to Off to prevent Windows from showing badges on taskbar buttons (such as the number of unread messages in the Mail app).

- **Taskbar location on screen.** Use this list to choose where you want to place the taskbar: Bottom, Left, Right, or Top. For example, if you want to maximize the available screen height, move the taskbar to the left or right side of the screen.

- **Combine taskbar buttons.** Use this list to choose how you want Windows to group taskbar buttons when an application has multiple windows or tabs open:

  - **Always hide labels.** Choose this option to have Windows always group similar taskbar buttons.

  - **When taskbar is full.** Choose this option to have Windows group similar taskbar buttons only when the taskbar has no more open space to display buttons.

  - **Never.** Choose this option to have Windows never group similar taskbar buttons.

Customizing the taskbar's notification area

The notification area appears on the right side of the taskbar, to the right of the icons for the running and pinned apps, as shown in Figure 1.7.

Task View   Show hidden icons

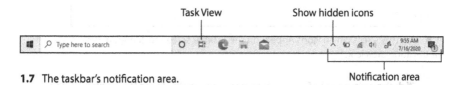

1.7 The taskbar's notification area.   Notification area

You can click the Show Hidden Icons button to see your hidden icons.

The notification area shows only a few icons by default: Network, Volume, and Notifications, and notebook PCs also show the Power icon. You might want to customize the default arrangement. For example, many notification icons offer quick access to their programs' features when you right-click them. If there is an icon that you right-click frequently, you might want to configure the notification area to show the icon on the taskbar. Here are the steps to follow:

1. **In the taskbar's Search box, type** select.

2. **In the search results, click Select Which Icons Appear on the Taskbar.** The Settings app displays the Select Which Icons Appear on the Taskbar screen, as shown in Figure 1.8.

13

← Settings — □ ✕

⌂ Select which icons appear on the taskbar

Always show all icons in the notification area
⊙ Off

Power
1 hr 12 min to full charge   ⊙ On

Network
LogophiliaS Internet access   ⊙ On

Volume
Speakers: 3%   ⊙ On

Windows Explorer
Bluetooth Devices   ⊙ Off

Windows Security notification icon
Windows Security - No actions nee...   ⊙ Off

Microsoft OneDrive
OneDrive Online   ⊙ Off

SkypeBridge
Skype - Signed In   ⊙ Off

Location Notification
Your location is currently in use   ⊙ Off

Microphone
Your assistant is ready to respond   ⊙ On

1.8 Use the Select Which Icons Appear on the Taskbar screen to configure your notification area icons.

3. **Click the switch to On for each icon you want to display in the notification area.**

Note

If you want to show every icon on the taskbar, click the Always Show All Icons in the Notification Area switch to On.

4. **Click the Back arrow in the top-left corner of the Settings window.** Settings takes you to the Taskbar screen.

5. **Click Turn System Icons On or Off.** Settings opens the Turn System Icons On or Off screen, shown in Figure 1.9.

6. **Click the switch to Off for each system icon you want to prevent from appearing in the notification area.** Windows puts the new settings into effect.

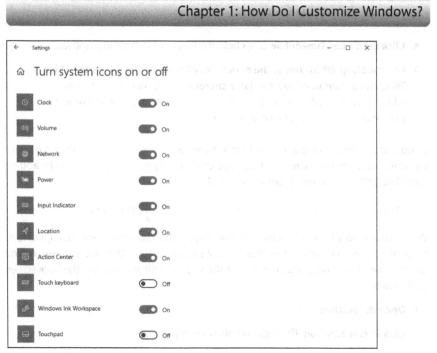

1.9 Use the Turn System Icons On or Off screen to toggle the display of system icons in the notification area.

Customizing the Lock Screen

Locking your computer is a useful safety feature because it prevents unauthorized users from accessing your files and your network. There are two main ways to lock your computer:

- Open the Start menu, click your user icon on the left side of the menu, and then click Lock.

- Press Windows+L.

Rather than remembering to lock your computer, you can configure Windows to automatically lock the computer after it has been idle for a specified amount of time. Here are the steps to follow:

1. **Open the Settings app.**

2. **Click Personalization.** The Personalization settings appear.

3. **Click Lock Screen.** The Lock Screen settings appear.

4. **Click the Screen Timeout Settings link.** The Power & Sleep settings appear.

5. **Use the Sleep list to choose the number of minutes of idle time after which Windows puts your PC to sleep (and, therefore, locks the PC).** If you have a tablet or notebook PC, be sure to set the sleep timeout both for when your PC is plugged in and when it is on battery power.

If you find yourself looking at the Lock screen frequently, you can improve the experience by customizing the Lock screen in two ways: by changing the background and by adding apps. The next two sections provide the details.

Changing the Lock screen background

You can make your Lock screen more interesting by changing the image that appears as its background. Windows comes with several system pictures that you can use, or you can use one of your own photos. Here are the steps to follow to change the Lock screen background:

1. **Open the Settings app.**

2. **Click Personalization.** The Personalization settings appear.

3. **Click Lock Screen.** The Lock Screen settings appear, as shown in Figure 1.10.

1.10 Use the Lock Screen settings to change the background image you see when you lock your PC.

4. **Use the Background list to choose Picture.** If you want to use a series of Microsoft Bing photos as the Lock screen background, click Windows Spotlight, instead.

5. **To use a system image, click the thumbnail of the picture that you want to use.** You can skip the rest of these steps.

6. **To use one of your own pictures, instead, click Browse.** The Open dialog box appears.

7. **Click the picture that you want to use.**

8. **Click Choose Picture.** The image appears the next time that you lock your computer.

Adding an app to the Lock screen

When you lock your PC, Windows displays status icons for some apps. For example, the status icon for the Mail app shows the number of unread messages. The Lock screen also shows any new notifications that appear for the Calendar app, such as an upcoming appointment. If you lock your computer frequently, you can make the Lock screen even more useful by adding icons for other apps, including ones that support notifications.

Before getting started, you need to understand the difference between a quick status and a detailed status on the Lock screen:

- **Quick status.** This means that the Lock screen shows only a small icon for an app, and that icon displays some sort of indication that you have new, unread, or pending items in the app. For example, the Mail app shows the number of unread email messages. You can display a quick status for up to seven apps.

- **Detailed status.** This means that the Lock screen shows more information from the app. For example, if you have an upcoming event in the Calendar app, the Lock screen shows the details of that event, including the event title, location, and time. You can display the detailed status for only a single app.

Follow these steps to control which applications appear on the Lock screen:

1. **Open the Settings app.**

2. **Click Personalization.** The Personalization settings appear.

3. **Click Lock Screen.** The Lock Screen settings appear.

4. **To choose which app displays its detailed status, click the button that appears under the Choose One App to Show Details Status on the Lock Screen heading, then choose an app from the list that appears.** If you don't want to see a detailed status, click None.

5. **To set a quick status icon for an app, click a button that appears under the Choose Which Apps Show Quick Status on the Lock Screen heading, then choose an app from the list that appears.** If you don't want an app associated with the icon, you can click None.

6. **Repeat Step 5 to set the other quick status icons.** Windows puts the new settings into effect, and the apps will now appear on the Lock screen.

Extending Your Desktop with Multiple Monitors

If you have a second monitor or even an extra TV that's relatively modern, you can improve your productivity and efficiency by connecting that display to your PC. To work with an extra monitor, you need two things (besides the extra monitor):

- Your PC must have an unused video output port that's compatible with the video input port on the monitor.
- A compatible cable to connect the ports.

There are many different types of video ports. However, all modern PCs and monitors (including TVs) use HDMI ports connected with an HDMI cable.

After you've connected your PC and the external monitor, you then need to configure Windows to extend the desktop to the second monitor.

Here are the steps to follow to connect and set up a second monitor:

1. **Connect the second monitor to your PC.** That is, you perform the following general steps:

   a. Connect one end of the cable to the compatible port on the back of the monitor.

   b. Connect the other end of the cable to the compatible port on the back of your PC.

2. **Open the Settings app and click System.** The System settings appear.

3. **Click Display.** The Display settings appear.

4. **Use the Multiple Displays list to choose Extend These Displays, as shown in Figure 1.11.** Windows asks you to confirm the display changes.

← Settings	— □ ×
⌂ Home	Display
Find a setting 🔍	Rearrange your displays
System	Select a display below to change the settings for it. Press and hold (or select) a display, then drag to rearrange it.
⬜ Display	
◁) Sound	
⬜ Notifications & actions	**1 2**
☽ Focus assist	
⏻ Power & sleep	
⬜ Battery	
⬜ Storage	Identify Detect
⬜ Tablet mode	Multiple displays
⬜ Multitasking	Multiple displays
⬜ Projecting to this PC	Extend these displays ⌄
	☑ Make this my main display

1.11 Use the Multiple Displays list to choose Extend These Displays.

5. **Click Keep Changes.**

6. **Click the monitor that you want to set as the main display.**

7. **Click Make This My Main Display.** Windows connects to the second monitor and uses the selected monitor as your main display.

Genius

After extending your desktop, you might find that your mouse pointer stops at the right edge of the left screen. This means that you need to swap the icons of the left and right monitors as they appear in the Display settings screen. To do that, drag the left monitor icon to the right of the other monitor icon (or vice versa).

Note

If you later decide you want to stop using the external monitor, follow Steps 2 and 3 in this section to open the Display settings, then use the Multiple Displays list to choose Show Only on 1. You can also usually revert to using just the original PC screen by disconnecting the monitor from your computer.

Setting Up Multiple Desktops

You can make your PC screen easier to manage and less cluttered by organizing your running programs into two or more desktops. Each desktop includes only the windows of the programs that you've assigned to that desktop. For example, you might have a work desktop that includes only a word processor, a spreadsheet, and Microsoft Edge for research; a social desktop that includes only Mail, People, and Calendar; and a media desktop that includes only Music, Photos, and Videos. You can quickly switch from one desktop to another.

Adding a new desktop

Here are the steps to follow to add another desktop to Windows:

1. **In the taskbar, click Task View.** I pointed out this icon earlier in Figure 1.7. You can also open Task View by pressing Windows+Tab.

2. **Click New Desktop.** Windows creates a new desktop. Windows names this Desktop 2 and your original desktop is named Desktop 1, as shown in Figure 1.12.

1.12 In the Task View screen, your desktops appear at the top, named Desktop 1, Desktop 2, and so on.

You can also create a new desktop by pressing Windows+Ctrl+D.

Switching to another desktop

The easiest way to populate a desktop is to switch to that desktop and then open the apps you want to run. Here are the steps to follow to switch to another desktop:

1. **In the taskbar, click Task View.** I pointed out this icon earlier in Figure 1.7. You can also press Windows+Tab.

2. **If you're not sure which desktop you want, you can see the apps running on a desktop by hovering the mouse pointer over the desktop.** Task View displays thumbnails of the desktop's running apps, as shown in Figure 1.13.

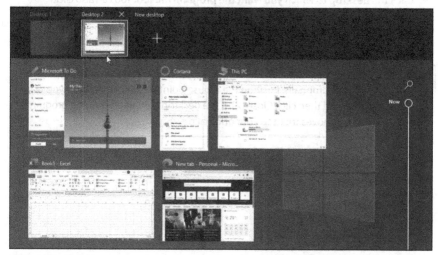

1.13 In the Task View screen, hover the mouse pointer over a desktop to see thumbnails of the desktop's running apps.

3. **Click the desktop you want to use.** Windows switches to that desktop and displays its running programs. Any new programs you launch will now appear only in the selected desktop.

21

Genius

You can also navigate the desktops without using Task View. Press and hold Windows+Ctrl, then press either the left arrow or right arrow key until you see the desktop you want, and then release all keys.

Moving an app to a different desktop

If an app is running in one desktop, but you'd prefer to have it running in a different desktop, following these steps to move it:

1. **In the taskbar, click Task View.** I pointed out this icon earlier in Figure 1.7. You can also press Windows+Tab.

2. **Right-click the app you want to move.**

3. **Click Move To.**

4. **Click the desktop to which you want the program moved.** You can also click New Desktop to move the program to a new desktop. Windows moves the program to the selected desktop.

Note

To close a desktop, click Task View (or press Windows+Tab) to display the desktop thumbnails. Position the mouse pointer over the desktop you want to close and then click Close (X). If the desktop contained running programs, Windows moves them to your original desktop.

How Can I Make the Most of Surfing the Web?

Settings × +

← → ↻ ⌂ ● Edge | edge://settings/appearance ☆ ⭐ ⊞ ● …

≡ **Settings** 🔍 Search settings

Customize browser

Default theme Light ∨

Zoom 100% ∨

Customize toolbar

Show home button
Set home page below

○ New tab page

● edge://newtab/ Save

Show favorites bar Only on new tabs ∨

Show favorites button

Show Collections button

Show feedback button

Show share button

With billions of pages covering every imaginable topic, the web is one of our greatest inventions and an unparalleled information source. To get at all that information, you need to take your web browsing to a higher level. In Windows, the default browser is Microsoft Edge, which is straightforward to use if all you do is click links and type addresses. But to get more out of the web, you need to tap into the impressive array of features and options that Edge offers. This chapter helps by showing you a few useful techniques that unleash the power of Edge.

Taking Advantage of Tabs 26

Saving Your Favorite Pages 30

Customizing Edge 34

Taking Advantage of Tabs

Like all modern web browsers, Edge supports *tabbed browsing*, which means you can open multiple websites at once in a single browser window. Each site appears in its own tab, and you can switch from one site to another just by clicking the tabs.

Opening a link in a new tab

Here are four popular ways to open a site in a new tab:

- **Right-click a link in a web page and then click Open Link in New Tab.** This creates a new tab and loads the linked page in the background (that is, you stay with your current page while the linked page loads in its tab).

- **Hold down Ctrl and click a link in a web page.** This creates a new tab and loads the linked page in the background.

- **Hold down Ctrl+Shift and click a link in a web page.** This creates a new tab and loads the linked page in the foreground. (That is, Edge immediately switches you to the new tab.)

- **Type the page address in the address bar and then press Alt+Enter.** This creates a new tab and loads the page in the foreground.

Creating a new tab

Rather than opening a linked page in a new tab, you can create a new tab first and then load the page you want into that tab. This is handy if you already know the address of the web page. There are two ways to create a new tab:

- Click the New Tab button, which is the + icon that appears to the right of the existing tabs (see Figure 2.1 in the next section).

- Press Ctrl+T.

With the new tab open and ready, type the web address in the address bar and then press Enter. This loads the page in the foreground.

Customizing the new tab page

When you create a new tab, as I describe in the previous section, Edge opens the new tab page, which offers a greeting to you, a Search the Web box, an image of the day, some quick links to pages you've visited recently, and links to stories from around the web. It's a real smorgasbord, but it might be ideal for you. If not, you can follow these steps to customize the new tab page:

1. **Open a new tab.**

2. **Click Page Settings.** This is the gear icon pointed out in Figure 2.1. Edge displays the new tab page settings.

New Tab button

Settings and More

Page Settings

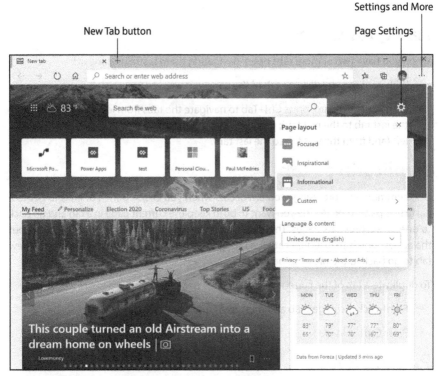

2.1 Click Page Settings to access the new tab page's customization features.

3. **Use the Page Layout section to click the type of content you want to see on the new tab page.** Your choices are Focused (which hides the image of the day and shows content with headings only), Inspirational, and Informational.

4. **For even more control over the layout, click Custom.** This enables you to toggle the quick links, the image of the day, and the greeting. You can also use the Content list to choose how you want the new tab page content displayed.

5. **To see content from another country (and to see the content in the language of that country), use the Language & Content list to choose which country you want to view.**

6. **Click Close (X).** Edge remembers your settings and uses them each time you create a new tab.

Navigating tabs

When you have two or more tabs open, navigating them is straightforward:

- With your mouse, click the tab of the page you want to use.

- With your keyboard, press Ctrl+Tab to navigate the tabs from left to right (and from the last tab to the first tab); press Ctrl+Shift+Tab to navigate the tabs from right to left (and from the first tab to the last tab).

Duplicating a tab

One common web browsing problem occurs when you click a bunch of links to get to a particular page, then decide you want to both keep the current page in a tab and go back to one of the previous pages. There are some convoluted solutions to this problem, but the easiest one is to just duplicate the tab of the current page. You can then use the new tab to go back to the previous page.

To duplicate a tab of the current page, you have two choices:

- Right-click the page's tab and then click Duplicate Tab.

- Press Ctrl+Shift+K.

Pinning a tab

If you have a web page that you visit often, you can save that page to Edge's Favorites list, as described later in this chapter. That's a useful way to store oft-surfed pages, but for your most-surfed pages, it would be better just to have Edge open that page in its own tab every time you launch the program.

That's easy enough to do by pinning a tab for that page, which tells Edge to create a permanent tab for it. You do this by right-clicking the page's tab and then clicking Pin Tab.

Controlling which tabs appear at startup

When you launch Edge, you see the new tab page. However, if you regularly view several different pages at the start of each Edge session, you can save time by opening those pages automatically each time you start Edge. Alternatively, you can configure Edge to reopen all the tabs you had running when you last closed the program.

Here are the steps to follow to configure what tabs appear when Edge starts:

1. **Click Settings and More.** This is the three-dot icon pointed out earlier in Figure 2.1. You can also press Alt+F.

2. **Click Settings.** Edge opens a new tab and displays the Settings page.

3. **Click Menu.** This is the three-horizontal-lines icon that appears near the top-left corner of the Settings page (it's pointed out in Figure 2.2). Note that you need to perform this step only when you're running Edge on a small screen.

2.2 Use the On Startup settings to specify what tab or tabs you want Edge to display each time you start the app.

4. **Click On Startup.** Edge opens the On Startup settings.

5. **Click a radio button:**

   - **Open a New Tab.** Edge starts up with just the new tag page (this is the default setting).

- **Continue Where You Left Off.** Edge starts up by reopening all the tabs you had running the last time you closed the program.

- **Open a Specific Page or Pages.** Edge starts up by displaying a page or pages you specify. You can click Use All Open Tabs to quickly add every running tab to the list. Otherwise, click Add a New Page, type the address of the page, and then click Add. Figure 2.2 shows the On Startup settings with a few pages added.

6. **Close the Settings tab.** Edge puts your settings into effect.

Closing tabs

To close a tab, Edge gives you a bunch of methods:

- Hover the mouse pointer over the tab and then click the tab's Close Tab (X) button.

- Click the tab and then press Ctrl+W.

- Right-click the tab and then click Close Tab.

- To close every tab except one, right-click the tab you want to keep open and then click Close Other Tabs.

- To close all the tabs you opened after a particular tab, right-click that tab and then click Close Tabs to the Right.

Genius

If you close a tab accidentally, you can get it back by right-clicking any open tab and then clicking Reopen Closed Tab. You can repeat this command as needed to reopen multiple tabs.

Saving Your Favorite Pages

If you have web pages that you visit frequently, you can save yourself time by storing links to those pages as favorites within Microsoft Edge. This enables you to display the pages with just a couple of clicks. You save favorite pages in Microsoft Edge by adding them to a special section of the app called the Favorites list. Instead of typing an address or searching for one of these pages, you can display the web page by clicking it in the Favorites list.

Adding a page to the Favorites list

When you come across a page you'd like to set up as a favorite, follow these steps to add the page to Edge's Favorites list:

1. **Display the web page you want to save as a favorite.**

2. **Click Add this Page to Favorites.** This is the icon pointed out in Figure 2.3. You can also choose this command by pressing Ctrl+D. The Favorite Added dialog box appears.

Add this Page to Favorites

Favorites

2.3 Click Add this Page to Favorites to place a page in Edge's Favorites list.

3. **Edit the page name, as necessary.** By default, the Name text box displays the title of the page, and this is the text that will appear when you view the list of your favorites later. Feel free to edit this text if you like.

4. **Use the Folder list to choose Other Favorites.**

5. **Click Done.** Microsoft Edge saves the web page as a favorite.

Genius

You can add all your open tabs as favorites by right-clicking any tab and then clicking Add All Tabs to Favorites (or by pressing Ctrl+Shift+D).

Working with the Favorites bar

One of Microsoft Edge's most useful features is the Favorites bar, which appears below the address box. The Favorites bar is fully customizable, which means you can populate the Favorites bar with new buttons associated with the sites you visit most often. This section shows you how to display and populate the Favorites bar and takes you through a few Favorites bar customizations.

Displaying the Favorites bar

Follow these steps to display the Favorites bar:

1. **Click Settings and More.** This is the three-dot icon pointed out earlier in Figure 2.1. You can also press Alt+F.

2. **Click Settings.** The Settings tab appears.

3. **Click Menu.** This is the three-horizontal-lines icon that appears near the top-left corner of the Settings page (it's pointed out earlier in Figure 2.2). The Settings menu appears. Note that you need to perform this step only when you're running Edge on a small screen.

4. **Click Appearance.**

5. **Use the Show Favorites Bar list to choose Always.** Microsoft Edge displays the Favorites bar.

6. **Click Close to close the Settings tab.**

Figure 2.4 shows the Favorites bar populated with a few favorites.

Favorites bar   Click here to access your other favorites

2.4 The Favorites bar gives you one-click access to some favorite pages.

Adding a web page to the Favorites bar

With the Favorites bar displayed, you can now add pages to it by following these steps:

1. **Navigate to the page you want to add to the Favorites bar.**

2. **Click Add this Page to Favorites.** I pointed out this icon earlier in Figure 2.3.

3. **Edit the page name, as necessary.**

4. **Use the Folder list to choose Favorites Bar.**

5. **Click Done.** Microsoft Edge adds the web page to the Favorites bar.

Genius

You can also create a Favorites bar button from a web page link. Navigate to the page that contains the link you want to add to the Favorites bar, drag the link text, and then drop it on the Favorites bar. A new button associated with the linked page appears on the Favorites bar.

Opening a page from the Favorites list

The purpose of the Favorites list, of course, is to give you quick access to the pages you visit regularly. To open one of the pages from your Favorites list, you have two choices:

- Click Favorites (pointed out in Figure 2.3), and then choose the favorite you want.

- If you added a page to the Favorites bar, click the favorite you want.

Genius

To open every page that you've saved to the Favorites bar, right-click the Favorites bar and then click Open All (*X*), where *X* is the number of items on the Favorites bar.

Maintaining favorites

When you have lots of favorites, you need to do some regular maintenance to keep things organized. This involves creating new subfolders, moving favorites between folders, changing addresses, deleting unused favorites, and more. Here's a summary of a few maintenance techniques you'll use most often:

- **Rename a favorite.** Display the Favorites list or the Favorites bar, and right-click the item you want to work with. Click Edit and then use the Name text box to adjust the name.

- **Change a favorite's address.** Display the Favorites list or the Favorites bar, and right-click the item you want to work with. Click Edit and then use the URL text box to adjust the address.

- **Move a favorite.** Display the Favorites list or the Favorites bar, and then drag the item to another spot in the list or bar.

- **Show only icons in the Favorites bar.** To create more room on the Favorites bar, display only web page icons by right-clicking any favorite and then clicking Show Icon Only.

- **Delete a favorite.** Display the Favorites list or the Favorites bar, right-click the item you want to work with, and then click Delete.

Customizing Edge

Microsoft Edge is a solid web browser that works well in its default state, but nobody ever got more productive by sticking with an app's default settings. We're all different and we all use and navigate the web in different ways. So, chances are that you'll find Edge easier and more pleasurable to use if you adjust a few customization options. The rest of this chapter shows you a few tweaks you can try.

Changing the Edge search engine

One of the handier features of Microsoft Edge is that it enables you to run web searches directly from the address bar. That is, you enter your search terms in the address bar, and then either click one of the suggested sites that Edge displays below the address bar, or press Enter to run the search (you can also press Alt+Enter to open the results in a new tab).

Note

To search for text within the current web page, press Ctrl+F (or click Settings and More and then click Find on Page) to open the Find on Page bar. Then type your search text. Edge highlights each instance on the page, and you can navigate these by clicking Next (the down arrow; you can also press Ctrl+G) or Previous (the up arrow; you can also press Ctrl+Shift+G).

By default, Edge initially submits the search text to the Bing search engine. Bing's a great search engine, but you might prefer to use a different search engine (such as Google). To change the Edge search engine, follow these steps:

1. **Click Settings and More.** This is the three-dot icon pointed out earlier in Figure 2.1. You can also press Alt+F.

2. **Click Settings.** The Settings tab appears.

3. **Click Menu.** This is the three-horizontal-lines icon that appears near the top-left corner of the Settings page (it's pointed out earlier in Figure 2.2). The Settings menu appears. Note that you need to perform this step only when you're running Edge on a small screen.

4. **Click Privacy and Services.**

5. **Scroll down to the Services section and click Address Bar.**

6. **In the Search Engine Used in the Address Bar list, choose the search engine you want Edge to use for address bar searches.** Figure 2.5 shows the available search engines. Depending on where you live, you might see a slightly different list.

7. **Click Close to close the Settings tab and put your new setting into effect.**

2.5 Use the Search Engine Used in the Address Bar list to tell Edge which search engine you prefer.

Changing the theme

You can change the overall look of Microsoft Edge by switching to a different theme. Here's how it's done:

1. **Click Settings and More.** This is the three-dot icon pointed out earlier in Figure 2.1. You can also press Alt+F.

2. **Click Settings.** The Settings tab appears.

3. **Click Menu.** This is the three-horizontal-lines icon that appears near the top-left corner of the Settings page (it's pointed out earlier in Figure 2.2). The Settings menu appears. Note that you need to perform this step only when you're running Edge on a small screen.

4. **Click Appearance.**

5. **Use the Default Theme list to choose the theme you want to use.** Figure 2.6 shows the available choices.

6. **Click Close to close the Settings tab and put your new setting into effect.**

2.6 Use the Default Theme list to change the Edge appearance.

Setting the default zoom level

If your eyesight is impaired or just not what it used to be, you might use the Zoom feature to increase the magnification of the sites you visit. To give this a try, click Settings and More, then use the Zoom buttons (pointed out in Figure 2.7) to set the magnification:

- **Click Zoom In (+) to increase the magnification.** You can also press Ctrl++ (plus).

- **Click Zoom Out (–) to decrease the magnification.** You can also press Ctrl+– (minus).

When you change the magnification for a page, Edge conveniently remembers the new setting and applies it to the page the next time you visit.

2.7 Use the Zoom buttons to change the magnification of the current web page.

That's a nice feature, but if you find yourself changing the Zoom magnification for all or most of the sites you visit, then you can make your life much easier by changing the default Zoom level that Edge applies to each site. Here are the steps to follow:

1. **Click Settings and More.** This is the three-dot icon pointed out earlier in Figure 2.1. You can also press Alt+F.

2. **Click Settings.** The Settings tab appears.

3. **Click Menu.** This is the three-horizontal-lines icon that appears near the top-left corner of the Settings page (it's pointed out earlier in Figure 2.2). The Settings menu appears. Note that you need to perform this step only when you're running Edge on a small screen.

4. **Click Appearance.**

5. **Use the Zoom list to choose the magnification level you want to use as the default.** Edge immediately applies the new setting to your open tabs. Note, though, that Edge does *not* apply the new setting to any tab in which you've previously set a custom Zoom level.

6. **Click Close to close the Settings tab.** Edge will now apply the new Zoom setting to each site you visit. Although, again, Edge won't apply the new Zoom level to any site for which you've previously set a custom Zoom level.

Customizing the toolbar

I discuss earlier in this chapter how you can display the Favorites bar. The Favorites bar appears just below the Edge toolbar, making it an example of a toolbar customization. Edge offers several other settings that you can use to set up the toolbar the way you prefer. Here are the steps to follow:

1. **Click Settings and More.** This is the three-dot icon pointed out earlier in Figure 2.1. You can also press Alt+F.

2. **Click Settings.** The Settings tab appears.

3. **Click Menu.** This is the three-horizontal-lines icon that appears near the top-left corner of the Settings page (it's pointed out earlier in Figure 2.2). The Settings menu appears. Note that you need to perform this step only when you're running Edge on a small screen.

4. **Click Appearance.**

5. **In the Customize Toolbar section (see Figure 2.8), use the following switches to customize the toolbar:**

   • **Show Home Button.** Toggles the Home button (pointed out in Figure 2.8). If you leave this switch On, choose one of the two radio buttons below the switch: Either click the New Tab Page radio button to open the new tab page when you click Home, or click the other (unnamed) radio button and enter the address of the page you want to see when you click Home.

Home button

2.8 Use the switches and other settings in the Customize Toolbar section to configure the Edge toolbar.

- **Show Favorites Bar.** As I described earlier, use this list to display or hide the Favorites bar.

- **Show Favorites Button.** Click this switch to Off to remove the Favorites button from the toolbar. This is useful if you only use the Favorites bar to access your favorites sites.

- **Show Collections Button.** Click this switch to Off to remove the Collections button (which appears to the right of the Favorites button). A *collection* is a set of web pages that you can work with as a group (say, by opening all the pages at once). If you don't use collections, then hiding the Collections button is a good idea.

- **Show Feedback Button.** Click this switch to On to add the Send Feedback button to the toolbar. Clicking this button enables you to report Edge problems to Microsoft.

- **Show Share Button.** Click this switch to On to add the Share button to the toolbar. Clicking this button enables you to send the address of the current page to a contact or to an app such as Mail, Skype, or OneNote.

6. **Click Close to close the Settings tab.**

Customizing the font

If you're having trouble reading most web pages, you can configure Edge to display text at a larger size and you can set a minimum type size. Similarly, you can also define default typefaces that will appear on web pages that don't specify their own fonts (which is, admittedly, rare these days). Here are the steps to follow to set these Edge font options:

1. **Click Settings and More.** This is the three-dot icon pointed out earlier in Figure 2.1. You can also press Alt+F.

2. **Click Settings.** The Settings tab appears.

3. **Click Menu.** This is the three-horizontal-lines icon that appears near the top-left corner of the Settings page (it's pointed out earlier in Figure 2.2). The Settings menu appears. Note that you need to perform this step only when you're running Edge on a small screen.

4. **Click Appearance.**

5. **Use the Font Size list to choose the relative font size you want to use as the default.** Your options are Very Small, Small, Medium, Large, and Very Large.

6. **Click Customize Fonts.** Edge opens the Customize Fonts page, shown in Figure 2.9.

2.9 Use the settings in the Customize Fonts page to configure the default font size and typefaces that Edge uses.

7. **Use the Font Size slider to set the default font sizes.** As you drag the slider, the numbers (and example sentences) below each of the four default font types (Standard Font, Serif Font, and so on) change accordingly.

8. **Use the Minimum Font Size slider to set the smallest font size you want Edge to use.** For example, if you set the minimum to 16 points and you surf to a web page that uses 14-point type, Edge will display the type using a 16-point font.

9. **For each of the four default font types—Standard Font, Serif Font, Sans-Serif Font, and Fixed-Width Font—use the associated list to choose the typeface you prefer.**

10. **Click Close to close the Settings tab.** Edge will now apply the new font settings to each site you visit. Note, however, that these settings will only work on sites that either don't specify their own typographic styles or that use typography based on Edge's default fonts.

How Do I Maximize Sending and Receiving Email?

Account settings   ×

Gmail sync settings

Download new content

| as items arrive | ∨ |

☑ Always download full message and Internet images

Download email from

| the last 3 months | ∨ |

Sync options

Email

⬤ On

Calendar

⬤ On

Contacts

⬤ On

🖫 Done   ✕ Cancel

Email is easy. Even novice computer users seem to grasp the basics of email quickly and are often sending messages within minutes. But if, like most people, you use email all day long, you probably want to make it even easier. This chapter shows you how to do that. The tasks you learn here are designed to shave precious seconds and minutes off everyday email chores. That may not sound like much, but added up over the course of a busy email day, those seconds can make the difference between leaving work on time and staying late.

Managing Mail Accounts **44**

Setting Options for Incoming Messages **47**

Setting Send Options. **51**

Managing Mail Accounts

Let's begin your email efficiency updates with a look at a few useful chores related to email accounts, including adding more accounts to Mail, changing the account name, and deleting accounts you no longer need.

Adding an account

Before you can send an email message, you must add your email account to the Mail app. This also enables you to use Mail to retrieve the messages that others have sent to your account.

You use Mail to set up email accounts with web-based services such as Gmail, as well as for POP (Post Office Protocol) and IMAP (Internet Message Access Protocol) accounts. Note, however, that if you're already signing in to Windows using a Microsoft account, then Windows automatically adds that account to the Mail app—so you need to follow the steps in this section only if you want to add another account to Mail.

Adding a web-based email account

Here are the steps to follow to add a web-based account service such as Outlook.com, Hotmail, Microsoft 365, Gmail, Yahoo!, and iCloud:

1. **Open the Mail app.** If you're starting Mail for the first time and the app prompts you to add an account, skip to Step 4.

2. **Click Settings.** This is the gear icon that appears in the lower-left corner of the Mail window. The Settings pane appears.

3. **Click Manage Accounts.** The Manage Accounts pane appears.

4. **Click Add Account.** The Add an Account dialog box appears, as shown in Figure 3.1.

5. **Click the type of account that you want to add.** Mail asks for your account email address.

3.1 Use the Add an Account dialog box to choose what type of account you want to add to Mail.

Note

How you proceed from here depends on the type of account you chose in Step 5. The steps that follow apply to most account types.

6. **Type your email address and then click Next.** Mail asks for your account password.

7. **Type your email password and then click Next or Sign In.** Mail asks for permission to access your account. Figure 3.2 shows the permission dialog box for a Gmail account.

Connecting to a service   ✕

G   Sign in with Google

Windows wants to access your
Google Account

🔵 pmcfedries@gmail.com

This will allow Windows **to:**

M   Read, compose, send, and permanently delete all   ⓘ
     your email from Gmail

👤   See, edit, download, and permanently delete your   ⓘ
     contacts

📅   See, edit, share, and permanently delete all the   ⓘ
     calendars you can access using Google Calendar

Cancel   Allow

3.2 For some email services, such as Gmail shown here, you must give Mail permission to access your account.

8. **Click Allow.**

9. **Click Done.** Mail adds your email account to the Accounts pane.

Adding a POP or IMAP account

POP and IMAP accounts used to require extensive setup that included entering the names of incoming and outgoing email servers, port numbers, and more. Fortunately, Mail is pretty good at ferreting out those details based on just your email address and password, so setting up a POP or IMAP account now requires just the following steps:

1. **Click Settings.** This is the gear icon that appears in the lower-left corner of the Mail window. The Settings pane appears.

2. **Click Manage Accounts.** The Manage Accounts pane appears.

3. **Click Add Account.** The Add an Account dialog box appears.

4. **Click Other Account.** The Other Account dialog box appears. Figure 3.3 shows a filled-in version.

5. **Type your email address, a name to display on sent messages, and your email password, and then click Sign In.** Mail locates your email service based on your address and then configures your POP or IMAP account automatically.

Add an account	×

Other account

Some accounts require additional steps to sign in.
Learn more

Email address

mail@mcfedries.com

Send your messages using this name

Paul McFedries

Password

••••••••••••

We'll save this information, so you don't have to sign in every time.

✓ Sign in   ✕ Cancel

3.3 Begin by providing Mail with your POP or IMAP account's address, name, and password.

Note

If Mail can't locate or access your email service, you'll see additional dialog boxes that prompt you for the account details, including the names of your account's incoming and outgoing email servers, the port numbers used by each server, and whether the connection is encrypted. Contact your email provider for this info.

Changing the account name

When you add two or more accounts to Mail, it's important that you can easily distinguish between each account. The easiest way to do that is to give each account a unique and easily recognizable name. For example, many people use the account's email address as the name. Here are the steps to follow to change an account's name:

1. **Click Settings.** This is the gear icon that appears in the lower-left corner of the Mail window. The Settings pane appears.

2. **Click Manage Accounts.** The Manage Accounts pane appears.

3. **Click the account you want to rename.** The Account Settings dialog box appears. Figure 3.4 shows an example.

4. **Use the Account Name text box to enter the name you prefer to use.**

5. **Click Save.** Mail renames the account and the new name appears in the Manage Accounts pane.

Deleting an account

To reduce clutter in the Mail app, you should remove any account that you no longer use or that is no longer active. Here are the steps to follow:

Account settings	×

Mcfedries account settings

✉ mail@mcfedries.com

Account name

| Mcfedries | × |

Change mailbox sync settings
Options for syncing your content.

Delete account from this device
Remove this account from this device.

🖫 Save   × Cancel

3.4 Use the Account Settings dialog box to rename an account.

1. **Click Settings.** This is the gear icon that appears in the lower-left corner of the Mail window. The Settings pane appears.

2. **Click Manage Accounts.** The Manage Accounts pane appears.

3. **Click the account you want to remove.** The Account Settings dialog box appears.

4. **Click Delete Account from this Device.** Mail asks you to confirm the removal.

5. **Click Delete.** Mail deletes the account.

6. **Click Done.**

Setting Options for Incoming Messages

Mail offers a few options for controlling and displaying your incoming messages. If you find your Inbox is getting harder to manage, perhaps some of the techniques I outline in the next few sections can help.

Customizing account sync settings

By default, Mail lets you know when you've received a new message as soon as the message arrives on the server. That's probably the best way to receive email, but if you're in no hurry, then you can configure Mail to check for new messages either at a specified time or whenever you feel like it. Here's how it's done:

1. **Click Settings.** This is the gear icon that appears in the lower-left corner of the Mail window. The Settings pane appears.

2. **Click Manage Accounts.** The Manage Accounts pane appears.

3. **Click the account you want to configure.** The Account Settings dialog box appears.

4. **Click Change Mailbox Sync Settings.** Mail displays the Sync Settings dialog box for the account. Figure 3.5 shows the dialog box for a Gmail account. Which settings are enabled in this dialog box depends on the type of account. For example, on most web-based accounts you should see all the settings enabled, while for a POP or IMAP account the Calendar and Contacts switches might be disabled.

Account settings	✕
Gmail sync settings	

Download new content

| as items arrive | ⌄ |

☑ Always download full message and Internet images

Download email from

| the last 3 months | ⌄ |

Sync options

Email
🔵 On

Calendar
🔵 On

Contacts
🔵 On

🖫 Done   ✕ Cancel

3.5 Use the Sync Settings dialog box to configure how often Mail checks for incoming messages.

5. **Use the Download New Content list to choose when you want Mail to check for new messages.** Besides the default As Items Arrive option, you can also choose a time (Every 15 Minutes, Every 30 Minutes, or Hourly), or you can choose Manually to check for new messages yourself.

6. **Use the Download Email From list to choose how far back you want Mail to download messages.** Choose Any Time to download all your messages; otherwise, choose a time such as The Last 3 Days, The Last Month, or The Last 3 Months.

7. **Click Done.**

8. **Click Save.** Mail saves your new settings.

Combining the Focused and Other tabs

By default, Mail separates your incoming messages into two tabs:

- **Focused.** These are the messages that, in Mail's estimation, are the most important to you.

- **Other.** All your supposedly non-important messages appear in this tab.

In theory, this is a great way to configure your Inbox: With all your important messages separated into their own tab, you can take care of those emails first and then switch to the less pressing stuff in the Other tab. In practice, however, you might find that Mail just doesn't do a great job of figuring out what's important to you. The result is that you often have to switch between Focused and Other to find the message you want, making you *less* efficient in the long run. If that happens to you, follow these steps to combine Focused and Other into a single Inbox tab:

1. **Click Settings.** This is the gear icon that appears in the lower-left corner of the Mail window. The Settings pane appears.

2. **Click Focused Inbox.** The Focused Inbox pane appears.

3. **If you have multiple accounts added to Mail, use the Select an Account list to choose which account you want to work with.**

4. **Click the Sort Messages into Focused and Other switch to Off, as shown in Figure 3.6.**

< Focused inbox

Select an account

Outlook   ∨

Sort messages into Focused and Other
 ◉) Off

3.6 For a unified Inbox, click the Sort Messages into Focused and Other switch to Off.

5. **Click Back (<) in the top-left corner of the Focused Inbox pane (or click outside the pane).** Mail combines the Focused and Other tabs into a unified Inbox.

Grouping messages individually

By default, Mail groups incoming messages by conversation. A *conversation* consists of an initial email message and then all the replies to the message, the replies to those replies, and so on. If you find that you have many long email conversations involving a large number of people, grouping your messages by conversation probably makes sense. Otherwise, you might find that grouping messages actually makes it harder to find the messages you want. If grouping messages by conversation is slowing you down, follow these steps to turn off this feature:

1. **Click Settings.** This is the gear icon that appears in the lower-left corner of the Mail window. The Settings pane appears.

2. **Click Message List.** The Message List pane appears.

3. **In the Organization section, choose the Individual Messages radio button, as shown in Figure 3.7.** Mail puts the new setting into effect immediately and no longer organizes your messages by conversation.

Controlling notifications

When a new message arrives in your Inbox, Mail lets you know by displaying a notification in the lower-right corner of the screen. (This is called a *notification banner*.) These notifications are handy if you're expecting an important message, but the rest of the time they can be real productivity killers (since they take your attention away from whatever you're working on). This is particularly true if the notification banner is accompanied by a sound.

< Message list

Swipe left

Archive ⌄

Organization

How do you want your messages to be organized?

● Individual messages

○ Grouped by conversation

3.7 To no longer group messages by conversation, choose the Individual Messages radio button.

To protect your precious attention from the onslaught of Mail's relentless notifications, follow these steps:

1. **Click Settings.** This is the gear icon that appears in the lower-left corner of the Mail window. The Settings pane appears.

2. **Click Notifications.** The Notifications pane appears.

3. **If you have multiple accounts added to Mail, use the Select an Account list to choose which account you want to work with.** Alternatively, if you want your new settings to apply to every account you've added to Mail, click the Apply to All Accounts check box.

4. **If you want to shut down all Mail notifications, click the Show Notifications in the Action Center switch to Off.** Otherwise, leave this switch On and customize the notifications as I describe in the next two steps.

5. **To prevent Mail from displaying notification banners, clear the Show a Notification Banner check box.** When you clear this check box, Mail automatically disables the Play a Sound check box, as shown in Figure 3.8.

< Notifications

Notification settings can be customized for each of your accounts.

Select an account

Outlook ⌄

☐ Apply to all accounts

Show notifications in the action center

⬤ On

☐ Show a notification banner

☑ Play a sound

☐ Show notifications for folders pinned to Start

3.8 To prevent Mail from pestering you with notifications, clear the Show a Notification Banner check box.

Even though the Play a Sound check box is still "checked," the fact that it's disabled means you won't hear a sound when messages arrive.

6. **To prevent Mail from playing a sound when a new message arrives, clear the Play a Sound check box.** You can only clear this check box if the Show a Notification Banner check box is clicked.

7. **Click Back (<) in the top-left corner of the Notifications pane (or click outside the pane).** Mail puts your new notification settings into effect.

Expand/Collapse

Switching between accounts

If you've configured Mail with two or more accounts, it's not obvious how you switch to another account to read that account's messages. Fortunately, switching to another account requires just a couple of steps:

1. **Click Expand/Collapse, which is the icon near the top-left corner of the Mail window that consists of three horizontal lines, as pointed out in Figure 3.9.**

2. **Click the account you want to use.** Mail switches to that account and displays the account's inbox.

Setting Send Options

Sending a message in Mail is straightforward: Switch to the account you want to use (as I described earlier in this chapter), click New Mail (+), address and compose your message, and then click Send. However, Mail also offers a few extra sending features and settings that you might find useful. I cover these options in the sections that follow.

3.9 Click the Expand/Collapse icon to see your accounts.

Creating a signature

A *signature* is (usually) a few lines of text that are automatically added to the end of each sent email to provide contact information and other data. Mail provides a default signature—Sent from Mail for Windows 10—that redefines the word *boring*. To craft your own signature (or to control whether Mail uses a signature at all), follow these steps:

1. **Click Settings.** This is the gear icon that appears in the lower-left corner of the Mail window. The Settings pane appears.

2. Click Signature. The Email Signature dialog box appears, as shown in Figure 3.10.

Email signature

Select an account and customize your signature

Outlook

☐ Apply to all accounts

Use an email signature

◖◗ On

| **B** | *I* | U | A | Calibri (Body ∨ | 11 ∨ | ⌘ | 🖾 |

Sent from Mail for Windows 10

| Save | Cancel |

3.10 Use the Email Signature dialog box to define a custom signature for your outgoing messages.

3. **If you have multiple accounts added to Mail, use the Select an Account and Customize Your Signature list to choose which account you want to work with.** Alternatively, if you want your new signature to apply to every account you've added to Mail, click the Apply to All Accounts check box.

4. **Click the Use an Email Signature switch to Off if you don't want to use a signature (including Mail's default signature) and skip to Step 6.**

5. **In the large text box, delete the default Sent from Mail for Windows 10 text and replace it with the signature you want to use.**

6. **Click Save to put the new signature into effect.**

Setting the default message font

You can add visual interest and make your messages easier to read by formatting the message text. A plain email message is quick to compose, but it's often worth the extra time to add formatting to your text. For example, you can add bold or italic formatting to highlight a word or phrase. For regular mail text, however, if you find yourself continually changing the message font to the same configuration, you can save lots of time by customizing Mail to always use those font options as the default mail text. Mail supports a wide array of formatting options, including the font, font size, formatting such as bold and italic, and font color.

Caution

All these formatting options have their place, but be careful not to overdo it, or you may make your message *harder* to read. Note, too, that not every recipient will see your formatting or have your formatting displayed properly, which is another reason to keep things simple, font-wise.

Here are the steps to follow to configure a default font for the messages you send:

1. **Click Settings.** This is the gear icon that appears in the lower-left corner of the Mail window. The Settings pane appears.

2. **Click Default Font.** The Default Font dialog box appears, as shown in Figure 3.11.

Default Font

Select an account and customize your default font

| Outlook ⌄ |

☐ Apply to all accounts

| Reset |

| Calibri (Body ⌄ | 11 ⌄ | **B** | *I* | U̲ | A̲ |

Messages you write will look like this by default. You can also change the format of your message in a new message window.

| Save | Cancel |

3.11 Use the Default Font dialog box to define the font that Mail uses when you compose a message.

3. **If you have multiple accounts added to Mail, use the Select an Account and Customize Your Default Font list to choose which account you want to work with.** Alternatively, if you want your new default font to apply to every account you've added to Mail, click the Apply to All Accounts check box.

4. **Use the Font, Font Size, Bold, Italic, Underline, and Font Color controls to configure your default font.** The font options you choose are reflected in the same text that appears below the controls.

5. **Click Save to put the new default font into effect.**

Changing your message priority

If you're sending a message that has important information or that requires a fast response, set the message's priority to high. When the recipient receives the message, his or her email program indicates the high priority. For example, Mail indicates high-priority messages with a red exclamation mark. Alternatively, you can set the priority to low for unimportant messages so that the recipient knows not to handle the message immediately. Mail flags low-priority messages with a blue, downward-pointing arrow.

Here are the steps to follow to set the message priority:

1. **Click New Message (+).** Mail creates a new email message.

2. **Click the Options tab.**

3. **Click the priority you want to use: High Importance or Low Importance.** Figure 3.12 points out these buttons in the Options tab.

4. **Complete your message and then click Send.** Mail sends the message using the priority level you chose.

Low Importance

High Importance

3.12 In the Options tab, click either High Importance or Low Importance to set the message priority.

Running the spell-checker to eliminate message errors

Whether you use email for short notes or long essays, you can detract from your message if your text contains more than a few spelling errors. Sending a message riddled with spelling mistakes can also reflect poorly on you, whether the recipient is your boss, your colleague, a customer, or a recruiter.

To ensure your message is received in its best light, you should activate Mail's spell-checker. This tool then checks your text for errors each time you send a message and offers suggested replacements. You can also improve the spell-checker by letting it know about flagged words that you know are correct. This can happen with people's names, company names and products, jargon terms, and so on.

Follow these steps to run the spell-checker:

1. **Click New Message (+).** Mail creates a new email message.

2. **Address your message, add a Subject line, and then enter your message text.**

3. **Make sure the insertion point is within the message body, then click the Options tab.**

4. **Click Spelling.** Mail launches the spell-checker. If it finds a word that it thinks is misspelled, it highlights the word and displays options similar to those shown in Figure 3.13.

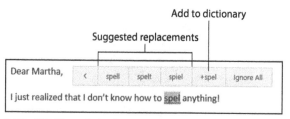

3.13 If Mail's spell-checker comes across a word it doesn't recognize, it highlights the word and displays some options for you.

5. **Handle the flagged word by using one of the following techniques:**

- Click one of the suggested replacements.

- Click +*word* (where *word* is the highlighted term) to add the word to the spell-checker's dictionary. This is the route to take for a word that you know is correct. By adding the word to the dictionary, you prevent the spell-checker from flagging the word in the future.

- Click Ignore All to have the spell-checker skip this and all other instances of the word.

6. **Repeat Step 5 until the spell check is complete.**

7. **Click Send.** Mail sends the message.

Can I Use Windows to Manage Contacts and Appointments?

You can use Windows to manage your social life. You can use the People app to store contact information such as email addresses, phone numbers, physical addresses, and birthdays. You can also work with contacts from other accounts, such as Gmail and iCloud, to help you keep track of all your friends, family, and business contacts. You can use the Calendar app to schedule meetings, appointments, and other events. You can quickly and easily add recurring events and get Calendar to remind you when an event is coming up.

Managing Your Contacts. 60

Tracking Your Events 71

Managing Your Contacts

You can easily store information about your friends, family, and colleagues, as well as send messages to them, by using the People app to add contacts from an existing account or create new contacts. Each contact can store a wide variety of information, such as a person's first and last names, company name, email address, phone number, and street address.

Adding contacts from an existing account

If you already have a list of contacts in another account, such as Microsoft 365, Gmail, or iCloud, you can add that account to the People app and get instant access to your contacts. To open the People app, click Start and then click People.

Adding Microsoft 365 contacts

Here are the steps to follow to add contacts from a Microsoft 365 (or Microsoft Exchange) account:

1. **In the People app, click Settings (the gear icon).** The Settings screen appears. If you don't see the Settings icon, click See More (the three dots pointed out later in Figure 4.2) and then click Settings.

2. **Click Add an Account.** The Add an Account dialog box appears.

3. **Click Office 365.** The People app prompts you for your Microsoft 365 login data.

Note

As this book went to press, Microsoft was in the process of renaming Office 365 to Microsoft 365. Therefore, note that by the time you read this, the Add an Account dialog box might show Microsoft 365 instead of Office 365.

4. **Type your Microsoft 365 email address and then click Next.**

5. **Type your Microsoft 365 account password and then click Sign In.**

6. **Click OK.** Windows adds your Microsoft 365 account.

7. **Click Done.** Windows syncs your Microsoft 365 contacts with the People app.

Adding Google contacts

Here are the steps to follow to add contacts from a Google account:

1. **In the People app, click Settings.** The Settings screen appears. If you don't see the Settings icon, click See More (the three dots pointed out later in Figure 4.2) and then click Settings.

2. **Click Add an Account.** The Add an Account dialog box appears.

3. **Click Google.** The People app prompts you for your Google login data.

4. **Type your Google email address and then click Next.**

5. **Type your Google account password and then click Next.** The People app shows you what it will do with your Google data.

6. **Click Allow.** Windows adds your Google account to your Microsoft account.

7. **Click Done.** Windows syncs your Google contacts with the People app.

Adding iCloud contacts

Here are the steps to follow to add contacts from an iCloud account:

1. **In the People app, click Settings.** The Settings screen appears. If you don't see the Settings icon, click See More (the three dots pointed out later in Figure 4.2) and then click Settings.

2. **Click Add an Account.** The Add an Account dialog box appears.

3. **Click iCloud.** The People app prompts you for your iCloud login data.

4. **Type your iCloud email address and password.**

5. **Click Sign In.** Windows adds your iCloud account to your Microsoft account.

6. **Click Done.** Windows syncs your iCloud contacts with the People app.

Controlling third-party content

When you add an account such as Gmail or iCloud, Windows assumes you want to use not just the account's contacts in the People app, but also the account's email in the Mail app and the account's calendars in the Calendar app. Fortunately, you can configure the type of content to sync between the account and Windows by following these steps:

1. **In the People app, click Settings.** The Settings screen appears. If you don't see the Settings icon, click See More (the three dots pointed out later in Figure 4.2) and then click Settings.

2. **Click the account you want to modify.** The Account Settings dialog box appears.

3. **Click Change Mailbox Sync Settings.** People displays the *Account* Sync Settings dialog box (where *Account* is the name of the account you're modifying). Figure 4.1 shows the Account Settings dialog box for a Google account.

4. **In the Sync Options group, use the Email, Calendar, and Contacts switches to toggle each type of content on or off.** For example, if you only want to use the account for contacts, click the Email and Calendar switches to Off, as shown in Figure 4.1.

5. **Click Done.** People returns you to the Account Settings dialog box.

6. **Click Save.** People saves your new account settings.

4.1 Use the switches in the Sync Options group to specify which content you want to sync.

Creating a contact

If you don't have another account from which to import contacts, or if you meet some new friends and want to store their contact data, you can create new contacts from within the People app. Here are the steps to follow:

1. **In the People app, click New Contact.** This is the plus sign (+) pointed out in Figure 4.2. The New *Account* Contact screen appears, where *Account* is the name of the account in the Save To list. (Note that you only see this list if you have two or more accounts associated with the People app.)

2. **If you have multiple accounts added to People, use the Save To list to choose the account to which you want the new contact added.**

3. **Use the Name text box to enter the contact's full name.** To enter separate first and last names, or to enter other name-related info such as the contact's middle name or nickname, click Edit Name (the pencil icon pointed out in Figure 4.2), use the Edit Name screen to enter the data, and then click Done.

New Contact   See More   Edit Name

People   — ☐ ✕

Search 🔍   +   ...   New Outlook contact

                               Add
                               photo

                               Save to
                               Outlook   ⌄

                               Name
                               Pierre Hadit   ✎

                               Mobile phone ⌄

                               + Phone

To see more contacts, select "Filter contacts" and pick which accounts
you'll see.   Personal email ⌄

                               + Email

                               + Address

                               Save   Cancel

Enter the email address here   Enter the phone number here

Select the email type here   Select the phone type here

4.2 Click New Contact to open the screen for creating a contact.

4. To enter one or more phone numbers, follow these sub-steps:

a. Use the list pointed out in Figure 4.2 to choose the type of phone number that you want to enter.

b. Enter the contact's phone number.

c. To add another phone number, click + Phone and then repeat Steps a and b.

5. To enter one or more email addresses, follow these sub-steps:

a. Use the list pointed out in Figure 4.2 to choose the type of email address that you want to enter.

b. Enter the contact's email address.

c. To add another email address, click + Email and then repeat Steps a and b.

6. **To enter a physical address, click + Address, click the label you want for the address, and then, using the text boxes that appear, type the contact's Street Address, City, State/Province, ZIP/Postal Code, and Country/Region.**

7. **To add more data, click + Other, click the type of data you want to add, and then enter the data in the fields that appear.** You can add any of the following data types: Website, Company, Job Title, Office Location, Significant Other, Children, Birthday, Anniversary, or Notes.

8. **Click Save.** The People app creates the new contact.

Viewing contacts

After you've added contacts and/or connected your other accounts to Windows, you can use the People app to view your contacts. The information that you see when you view a contact depends on how the contact was added to Windows. If you added the contact yourself, you see the information that you entered. If the contact was added by connecting another account to Windows, you see the data provided by that account. If you have many contacts, you can also use the People app's Search feature to locate the contact you want to view.

Viewing a contact

Here are the steps to follow to view any contacts in the People app:

1. **Scroll the Contacts list up or down to locate the contact you want to view.** You can also click any of the letters that divide the Contacts list alphabetically. In the grid of letters that appears, click the letter you want to view.

Genius

By default, People sorts your contacts by first name. If that doesn't make much sense to you, click Settings (you might have to click See More, first; see Figure 4.2) to open the People app's Settings pane. In the Sort Contact List By section, click Last Name.

2. **Click the contact.** The People app displays the contact's data.

Searching for a contact

Here are the steps to follow to search for a contact in the People app:

1. **Click in the People app's Search box.**

2. **Begin typing the name of the contact you want to view.** People displays a list of contacts with names that match your typing.

3. **When you see the contact you want to view, click the name in the search results.** The People app displays the contact's data.

Editing a contact

If you need to make changes to the information already in a contact, or if you need to add new information to a contact, you can edit the contact from within the People app. While editing a contact, you can modify the existing information, add new information to the contact, or delete existing information. Follow these steps:

1. **In the People app, click the contact you want to edit.**

2. **Click Edit.** People makes the contact's fields available for editing.

3. **Edit the existing fields as required.**

4. **To add a field, click the + icon beside the field type you want to use and then type the data.**

5. **To remove a field, position the mouse pointer over the field and then click Remove (the X pointed out in Figure 4.3).**

6. **When you complete your edits, click Save.** People saves the edited contact.

Assigning a photo to a contact

You can add visual interest to the People app and make it more useful by assigning photos to your contacts. By default, the People app shows a standard image for each contact. For your Microsoft account, that image is a generic headshot, but other accounts have different images. For example, Google's images consist of just the contact's initials. Assigning photos not only improves the look of the People app, but it also helps you remember your contacts, particularly if they're business colleagues or similar acquaintances whom you don't see very often.

Follow these steps to assign a photo to a contact:

1. **In the People app, click the contact you want to work with and then click Edit.** People opens the contact for editing.

2. **Click Add Photo.** A scaled-down version of the Photos app appears and displays your photos.

Remove

Edit Outlook Contact

Add
photo

Name

Alex Blandman   ✎

Mobile phone ∨

1 555-703-3943

Work phone ∨   ✕

1 555-703-3993

+ Phone

Work email ∨

alexbl@boringdrills.com

+ Email

| Save | Cancel |

4.3 To delete a field, hover the mouse pointer over the field and then click the field's Remove icon.

3. **Click the photo you want to add.**
   Photos prompts you to choose the
   area of the photo that you want to
   use for the contact (see Figure 4.4).

4. **Click and drag the photo to set
   the area you want to use within
   the circle.**

5. **Click and drag any of the four
   handles to set the size of the
   circle.**

6. **Click Done.** People adds the photo
   to the contact.

7. **Click Save.** People saves the edited
   contact.

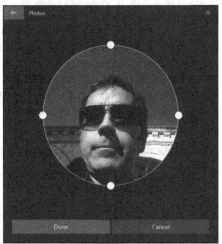

4.4 Use this window to choose the area of the image to use as the contact's photo.

66

Note To change a contact's photo, open the contact for editing, and then click the existing photo to open the Photos app and see your photos. Click the new photo you want to use and then follow Steps 4 to 7 to set the photo position and size and save your changes. To remove a photo, right-click it and then click Delete Photo.

Creating a new contact from an electronic business card

Entering a person's contact data by hand is a tedious bit of business at the best of times, so it helps if you can find a faster way to do it. If you can cajole a contact into sending his contact data electronically, then you can add it with just a couple of clicks. What do I mean when I talk about sending contact data electronically? Long ago, the world's contact-management gurus came up with a standard file format for contact data—the vCard. It's a kind of digital business card that exists as a separate file.

Note Unfortunately, the Mail app doesn't support the vCard file format, so you can't create a new contact from a vCard file you receive as an attachment. You can't even save the attachment, so you'll need to find some other way to get the vCard file stored on your PC or OneDrive to continue (for example, by using an online email app, such as Gmail, or by using a file-sharing service, such as Dropbox).

Assuming you've got a vCard file saved to your PC or your OneDrive, to get this data into your Contacts app, follow these steps:

1. **In File Explorer, right-click the vCard file.**

2. **Click Open With and then click People.** People opens the vCard, as shown in Figure 4.5.

3. **Click Save.** People creates a new contact from the info on the vCard.

4. **Edit the data or add data as required.**

5. **Click Save.** People saves the new contact.

Alex Blandman - People   —   □   ✕

AB   **Alex Blandman**

Contact   💾 Save

Mobile phone
1 555-703-3943   📞 Call with Skype   📞 Call with Your Phone

Work phone
1 555-703-3993   📞 Call with Skype   📞 Call with Your Phone

Work email
alexbl@boringdrills.com   ✉ Email

Home address
12 Prosaic Pathway   🗺 Map
Dull, IN 46290

See more >

4.5 A vCard file opened with the People app.

Filtering your contacts

You can make a long Contacts list easier to navigate and manage by filtering it to hide certain contacts. For example, if you mostly use People to locate contacts for phone calling or text messaging, you can filter the Contacts list to hide all those contacts who don't have a phone number. Similarly, if you have multiple accounts added to the People app, you might find that this creates many duplicate entries. You can fix this problem by filtering the Contacts list to hide all contacts from a particular account.

Hiding contacts without phone numbers

Follow these steps to filter your contacts to hide those who don't have a phone number:

1. **In the People app, click Filter Contacts.** The Filter Contacts dialog box appears. If you don't see the Filter Contacts icon, click See More (the three dots pointed out earlier in Figure 4.2) and then click Filter Contacts.

2. **Click the Hide Contacts Without Phone Numbers switch to On, as shown in Figure 4.6.**

3. **Click Done.** People only shows those contacts who have at least one phone number.

Hiding contacts by account

To hide the contacts from a particular account, follow these steps:

1. **In the People app, click Filter Contacts.** The Filter Contacts dialog box appears. If you don't see the Filter Contacts icon, click See More (the three dots pointed out earlier in Figure 4.2) and then click Filter Contacts.

2. **Clear the check box of the account you want to hide.**

3. **Click Done.** People hides the contacts from the account you cleared in Step 2.

Filter contacts

Hide contacts without phone numbers

On

Shows only the contacts you can call or text. You can still find the rest by searching.

Show contacts from

☑ Outlook (Mail and Calendar)

☐ Recent contacts (Microsoft People)

☑ Google (Mail and Calendar)

Done   Cancel

4.6 Turn on the Hide Contacts Without Phone Numbers switch to hide contacts that don't have phone numbers.

Linking multiple profiles to a contact

When you add multiple accounts to the People app, you might end up with the same contact listed two or more times. If those profiles contain different data—for example, one might contain personal information while the other contains work information—it's a hassle to try to remember which is which. A better alternative is to link those profiles, which tells People to display all the contact's data in a single profile.

Combining a suggested contact

In some cases, People will determine that two profiles are similar enough that it suggests that you combine the two profiles. Follow these steps to link a contact's suggested profile:

1. **In the People app, click one of the profiles that you want to link.** If the People app has found a similar contact, you see that contact's name in the Suggested section, as shown in Figure 4.7.

2. **Click Combine.** People asks you to confirm that you want to combine the contacts.

3. **Click Combine.** People combines the contacts into a single profile.

Note If the suggested contact is incorrect, you can click See More and try the steps in the next section.

Locating and combining a contact

To combine multiple profiles manually, follow these steps:

1. **In the People app, click one of the profiles that you want to link.**

2. **Click Find a Contact to Combine.** The Choose a Contact pane appears. If your Contacts list is long, you can use the Search box to locate the contact.

3. **Click the contact you want to combine.** People combines the contacts into a single profile.

Deleting a contact

If you no longer need a contact, you should delete it from the People app to reduce clutter in the Contacts list. Here are the steps to follow:

AB **Alexander Blandman**

Events
Upcoming events with this contact will show up here.

Conversations
Recent conversations with this contact will show up here.

Combined contacts

Suggested

Alex Blandman
Found in Outlook

Combine   Dismiss

How you're connected
Outlook

See more >

4.7 If People detects a similar contact profile, it displays a suggested contact for combining.

1. **Choose the contact you want to remove.**

2. **Click Delete (the trashcan icon).** You can also right-click the contact and then click Delete. The People app asks you to confirm.

3. **Click Delete.** People removes the contact.

Tracking Your Events

Windows comes with a Calendar app to enable you to manage your schedule. To create an event such as an appointment or meeting, or an all-day event such as a conference or trip, you choose the date when the event occurs.

Viewing your calendar

Calendar lets you change the calendar view to suit your needs. For example, you can show just a single day's worth of events if you want to concentrate on that day's activities. Similarly, you can view a week's or a month's worth of events if you want to get a larger sense of what your overall schedule looks like.

Changing the calendar view

Use the following techniques to change the calendar view:

- **Viewing events by month.** In the Calendar app toolbar, click Month. Your calendar for the month appears and you can click the up and down arrows to navigate the months (see Figure 4.8).

Menu   Navigation arrows

4.8 The Calendar app in Month view.

- **Viewing events by week.** In the Calendar app toolbar, click Week. Your events for the week appear and you can click the left and right arrows to navigate the weeks.

Genius

In Week view, if you prefer to see just Monday through Friday, pull down the Week list and click Work Week.

● **Viewing events by day.** In the Calendar app toolbar, click Day. The events for a single day appear and you can click the left and right arrows to navigate the days.

Genius

You can set up a custom Day view that shows one to six days at a time. Pull down the Day list and click the view you want: 1 Day, 2 Day, 3 Day, 4 Day, 5 Day, or 6 Day.

● **Viewing today's events.** In the Calendar app toolbar, click Today. The events for the current date appear.

Navigating with the mini calendar

You can navigate the calendar by using the mini calendar that appears on the left side of the Calendar window. If you don't see the mini calendar, click Menu in the upper-left corner of the Calendar window (pointed out in Figure 4.8). Use the mini calendar's up and down arrows to navigate the months, then click the day you want to view.

Adding an event to your calendar

You can help organize your life by using the Calendar app to record your upcoming events—such as appointments, meetings, phone calls, and dates—on the date and time that they are scheduled to occur.

If the event has a set time and duration—for example, a meeting or a lunch date—you add the event directly to the calendar as a regular appointment. If the event has no set time—for example, a birthday, anniversary, or multiple-day event such as a sales meeting or vacation—you can create an all-day event.

Creating a time-based event

Follow these steps to create an event that has a set time and duration:

1. **In the Calendar app, navigate to the date when the event occurs.**

2. **Click the time when the event starts.** If you're currently in Month view, click the day the event occurs. Calendar displays a window for you to enter the event details, as shown in Figure 4.9.

3. **Type a name for the event.**

4. **If the event times are incorrect, use the start and end controls to choose the correct times.** If you can't change the times, make sure the All Day check box is cleared.

5. **(Optional) Type the event location.**

6. **Click Save.** Calendar adds the event to your schedule.

To make changes to the event, you can click it.

Start time   End time

4.9 Use this window to enter the details of your event.

Creating an all-day event

Follow these steps to create an event that has no set time, such as an anniversary or conference:

1. **In the Calendar app, navigate to the date when the event occurs.**

2. **Click the time when the event starts.** If you're currently in Month view, click the day the event occurs.

3. **Type a name for the event.**

4. **Click the All Day check box.**

5. **(Optional) Type the event location.**

6. **Click Save.** Calendar adds the event to your schedule where it appears as a banner at the top of the date when you are in Day or Week view.

Creating a recurring event

If you have an activity or event that recurs at a regular interval, you can create an event and configure it to automatically repeat in the Calendar app. This saves you from having to repeatedly add the future events manually because Calendar adds them for you automatically.

You can repeat an event daily, weekly, monthly, or yearly. If your activity recurs every day only during the workweek, such as a staff meeting, you can also set up the event to repeat every weekday.

Follow these steps to set up a recurring event:

1. **Follow the steps in the previous section to create an event and then click the event.** Calendar displays the event info.

2. **Click More Details.** Calendar displays the event details screen.

3. **Use the Repeat list to click the repeat interval that you want to use.** You might also be able to further refine your choice, such as choosing the specific day of the week for the Weekly interval.

4. **If needed, use the End control to choose the last recurrence.**

5. **Click Save.** Calendar adds the future events using the interval that you specified.

Note

> To edit a recurring event, click any occurrence to open that event. You can edit just that occurrence or click Edit Series to edit every occurrence.

Adding an event reminder

You can help make sure that you never miss a meeting, appointment, or other event by setting up the Calendar app to remind you before the event occurs. A *reminder* is a notification message that Windows displays at a specified time before the event occurs. By default, Calendar adds a 15-minute reminder to each event, but you can change that to a more suitable interval.

Follow these steps to add a reminder to an event:

1. **Follow the steps shown earlier to create an event and then click the event.** Calendar displays the event info.

2. **Click More Details.** Calendar displays the event's details screen, shown in Figure 4.10.

3. **Use the Reminder list (pointed out in Figure 4.10) to choose the length of time before the event that you want the reminder to appear.**

4. **Click Save.** Calendar saves the event and later reminds you of it beforehand, according to the time that you chose.

Setting up an online meeting

The Calendar app has a feature that enables you to include people in an online meeting (using the Skype app) by sending them invitations to attend. The advantage of this

Reminder

Calendar							—
Home							
🔲 Save	🗑 Delete	🌐 Online meeting	Busy		15 minutes	⟳	🔒

Details

● ⌄ Event name   ● Calendar · Outlook ⌄
Location
3:00 PM ⌄   3:30 PM ⌄   ☐ All day
⟳ Every day, effective 8/23/2020 until 11/23/2020 from 3:00 PM to 3:30 PM

Repeat

Start: August 23, 2020 📅
Daily ⌄
● Every   1 ⌄ day(s)
◯ Every weekday
End: November 23, 2020 📅

4.10 The details screen for an event.

approach is that when other people respond to the invitation, Calendar automatically updates the event.

1. **Follow the steps shown earlier to create an event and then click the event.** Calendar displays the event info.

2. **Click More Details.** Calendar displays the event details screen, shown earlier in Figure 4.10.

3. **Click Online Meeting.**

4. **In the People section, use the Invite Someone text box to specify a person whom you want to invite:**

   ● If the person is in your People app, start typing the person's name, then click the person when the full name appears in the list of search results.

Genius

If you want to include quite a few people from the People app, an easier way to add them is to click the People icon that appears on the right side of the Invite Someone text box. In the People window that appears, click each person you want to invite and then click Done (the check mark).

   ● If the person isn't in your People app, type the person's email address and press Enter.

5. **Repeat Step 4 for each person you want to invite.**

Note

To remove a person from the invitation, you can move the mouse pointer over the person and then click Remove (X).

6. **Use the large, unlabeled text box to type a note that will appear with the invitation.**

7. **Click Send.** Calendar saves the event and sends the invitation.

When your meeting time arrives, click the event to open it, as shown in Figure 4.11, then click Join Online Meeting.

Calendar	—	□	×

Home   Format   Review

▷ Send   ⊠ Cancel   ⊕ Join online   ↶ Respond   Busy   15 minutes   ↻   🔒   🔍

Details

People

● ˅ Startup brainstorming session

Invite someone   ☒

Sort by   Original order   ˅

Location

Me
Organizer

Start: August 23, 2020   📅   1:00 PM   ˅   ☐ All day

Aardvark Sorenstam
asorenstam@whatever.com

End: August 23, 2020   📅   3:00 PM   ˅

Paul McFedries
pmcfedries@gmail.com

Pete Sellars
contact@logophiliapress.com

Join online meeting

alexbl@boringdrills.com
alexbl@boringdrills.com

alice@gibbbens.com
alice@gibbbens.com

Davida Sigurdsdottir
davidaig@bjork.com

4.11 To connect to your online meeting, open the event and then click Join Online Meeting.

Customizing your calendar

Calendar is a useful tool right out of the box, but it comes with a decent collection of customization settings that you can use to make the app even better. For example, you can specify a first day of the week other than Sunday. You can also specify which days are in your workweek and which hours are in your workday. You can also display week numbers and change the Calendar colors. Here are the steps to follow:

1. **Click Settings.** The Settings pane appears.

2. **Click Calendar Settings.** The Calendar Settings pane appears, as shown in Figure 4.12.

3. **Use the First Day of Week list to choose the day you prefer to use as the first of the week.**

4. **Use the Days in Work Week check boxes to define your workweek.**

5. **In the Working Hours section, use the Start Time and End Time lists to define the beginning and end of your workday.**

6. **If you want to display week numbers in the calendar, use the Week Numbers list to choose an option.** Besides the default option of Off, the Week Numbers list offers three numbering options:

   - **First Day Of Year.** Calendar designates week 1 as the week that contains January 1, even if that week contains one or more days from the previous year.

   - **First Full Week.** Calendar designates week 1 as the first full week that occurs in the year, even if the previous week contains one or more days from the current year.

   - **First Four-Day Week.** Calendar designates week 1 as the first week that contains at least four days of the new year, even if the week contains days from the previous year.

7. **Click outside the Calendar Settings pane to close the pane.** Calendar puts the new settings into effect.

< Calendar Settings

Week

First Day of Week

Sunday

Days in Work Week

☐ Sunday
✓ Monday
☑ Tuesday
☑ Wednesday
☑ Thursday
✓ Friday
☐ Saturday

Working Hours

Start time

8:00 AM

End time

4.12 Use the Calendar Settings pane to customize your calendar.

What Other Day-to-Day Tasks Can I Perform?

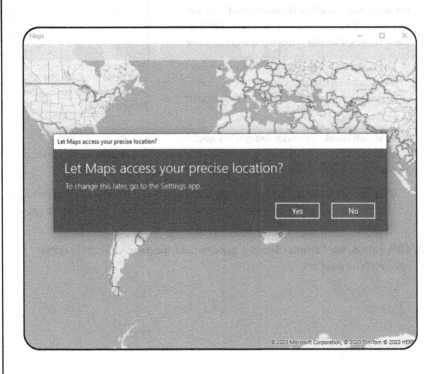

You can use the apps that come with Windows to perform a number of useful day-to-day tasks. For example, rather than looking through menus and folders to find apps, settings, and files, you can search for them, either by typing or by voice commands. Other useful tasks you can perform with Windows are getting directions to a location; looking up a weather forecast; performing calculations and conversions; recording voice memos; and setting alarms and timers. This chapter takes you through these tasks and more.

Finding Stuff on Your PC **80**

Configuring the Cortana Voice Assistant. **83**

Making Video Calls **85**

Working with Maps **87**

Checking the Weather **93**

Finding Stuff on Your PC

After you've used your PC for a while and have created many documents, you might have trouble locating a specific file. You can save a great deal of time by using the built-in tools and features of Windows to locate what you need.

Viewing your timeline

Windows comes with a Task View feature that includes a timeline of your recent activities, particularly documents you've opened recently. If the object you want to locate is a document you worked with in the past few days, you can open your timeline and click the document. Here are the steps to follow:

1. **In the taskbar, click the Task View icon.** This icon is pointed out in Figure 5.1. You can also run Task View by pressing Windows+Tab. The Task View screen appears, as shown in Figure 5.2.

Caution

When you first open Task View, you see the See More Days in Timeline text, which offers you 30 days of timeline activity if you click the Yes button. Note, however, that this means your activities are sent to and stored with Microsoft, so if you regularly view sensitive or private documents, think twice before accepting this offer.

2. **Scroll the timeline down until you see the document you want to use.**

3. **Click the document.** Windows launches the document's app, if it's not open already, and then switches to the document.

Task View

Talk to Cortana

5.1 Click the taskbar's Task View icon to open Task View and see your timeline.

Searching your PC

You can use the Search feature to look for apps, system settings, and documents on your PC, as well as websites on the Internet. If you're working with File Explorer, you can also perform document searches using the Search box in a folder window.

Using Multiple Desktops

You can make your PC screen easier to manage and less cluttered by organizing your running programs into two or more desktops. Each desktop includes only the windows of the programs that you have assigned to that desktop. For example, you might have a work desktop that includes only a word processor, a spreadsheet, and Microsoft Edge for research; a social desktop that includes only Mail, People, and Calendar; and a media desktop that includes only Music, Photos, and Videos. You can quickly switch from one desktop to another. To create another desktop, click the taskbar's Task View icon and then click New Desktop. (You can also press Windows+Ctrl+D to create a new desktop.) You can then use Task View to switch from one desktop to another. Alternatively, press and hold Windows+Ctrl, press the left arrow key or right arrow key until you see the desktop you want, and then release all the keys.

Windows displays thumbnails for each running program

Click and drag this button to scroll the timeline

Timeline activities

5.2 Use the Task View timeline to see your recent activities.

Searching from the taskbar

Here are the steps to follow to run a search from the Windows taskbar:

1. **Click inside the Search box and type your search text.** Windows displays the top apps, settings, and documents with names that include your search text. Figure 5.3 shows an example.

Note

There isn't a way to search for settings first, but the Settings app does have a search feature. Click Start, click Settings, and then use the Search box to type a word or phrase for the setting you want.

2. **To see results from a specific category, click a heading, such as Apps or Documents.** You can click More to see extra categories, such as Email and Folders.

3. **Click the item you want.** Windows opens the app, setting, document, or website.

Click More to see more categories

All Apps Documents Web More ▼	0 🔘 ₽ ···
Best match	
🖶 Printers & scanners System settings	🖶
Apps	Printers & scanners
🖶 Print 3D >	System settings
✂ Snipping Tool >	
Settings	◻ Open
🖶 Add a printer or scanner >	
🖾 Use the Print Screen key to launch screen snipping >	**Get quick help from web**
🖶 Let Windows manage my default printer >	Changing printer status
🖾 Change advanced color management settings for >	Downloading print drivers
🖾 Find and fix problems with printing >	Scanning documents
Search the web	
🔎 print - See web results >	
🔎 printers & scanners	○ 🖽 🥯 🗔 📧 ∧ 🖾 🕪

5.3 Type some text in the taskbar's Search box to see items that match what you type.

Searching from a folder window

Follow these steps to use File Explorer to search a folder:

1. **Launch File Explorer.** You can either click the File Explorer icon in the taskbar or click Start and then click Documents or Pictures.

2. **Open the folder you want to search.**

3. **Type your search text in the Search box.** As you type, Windows displays the folders and documents in the current folder with names, contents, or keywords that match your search text.

Genius

You can tell File Explorer to search only one of more than 20 different file types, including documents, music, and pictures. In File Explorer, click inside the Search box, enter your search text, and then press Enter. Click the Search tab in the Ribbon and then use the Kind list to choose the type of file you want to find.

4. **If you see the folder or document that you want, double-click it.** The folder or document opens.

Configuring the Cortana Voice Assistant

If you have a microphone attached to your PC, you can use it to search for information on your computer and on the web by using voice commands. To set up this feature, you need to configure Cortana, the Windows voice assistant. Cortana knows what's on your PC and what's available on the web. Although you can still type searches as described in the previous section, once Cortana is configured you can run searches and other tasks using verbal commands that you speak into your microphone.

Here are the steps to follow to configure Cortana:

1. **Click the taskbar's Talk to Cortana icon.** I pointed out this icon earlier in Figure 5.1. Cortana asks you to sign in.

2. **Click Sign In.** Windows asks you to choose an account to sign in to Cortana.

3. **Click the account you want to use (most likely your Microsoft account) and then click Continue.** Windows asks if you want to allow Cortana to access your account data.

4. **Click Yes.** Windows asks if you want to allow Cortana to access your personal data.

Caution

Cortana can easily end up storing a ton of data about you. If that makes you nervous, complete these steps and then click the Talk to Cortana icon (see Figure 5.4). Click Open Menu (the three dots), click Settings, click Privacy, and then use the settings that appear to clear your data.

5. **Click Accept and Continue.** You can now use Cortana to search and control your PC.

Controlling your PC with Cortana

You can use the Cortana voice assistant to control various aspects of your PC. These tasks include running apps and opening specific pages of the Settings app. You can also use Cortana to streamline aspects of your life. For example, you can use Cortana to set up reminders, create lists, send email, or access your calendar. You can perform any of these using either keyboard or voice instructions. Note, too, that Cortana gets more powerful with each new update of Windows, so the list of tasks you can perform with Cortana will grow over time.

Follow these steps to use Cortana voice commands to control your PC:

1. **Click the taskbar's Talk to Cortana icon.** I pointed out this icon earlier in Figure 5.1. The Cortana window appears.

2. **Click the Talk to Cortana icon, pointed out in Figure 5.4.** Cortana displays an animation to let you know it's listening for your voice command.

Cortana	—	□	×

...

○

Hi there, how can i help?

remind me to leave in 1 hour

I'll remind you.

Leave
Today • 2:43 PM

✔ Microsoft To Do   Edit in To Do

Ask Cortana   🎤

Talk to Cortana

5.4 An example Cortana command and its response.

Making Cortana Easier to Access

You can configure Cortana to respond to a *wake word*, which is a word that, when spoken into your PC's microphone, activates Cortana's speech recognition feature. The wake word is "Cortana." Open the Settings app, click Privacy, and then click Voice Activation. In the Choose Which Apps Can Use Voice Activation section, under the Cortana app, click the Cortana Starts Listening When You Say "Cortana" switch to On. You can also configure Cortana to recognize voice commands immediately after you press the keyboard shortcut Windows+C. Click Talk to Cortana, click Menu (the three dots), click Settings, and then click Talk to Cortana. In the Keyboard Shortcut Preference section, click the Speak or Type radio button.

3. **Speak your command or search text into your PC's microphone.** Cortana carries out your request. Figure 5.4 shows an example.

Making Video Calls

You can use the Skype app to place calls to friends and family using your Internet connection. Unlike regular phone calls, Skype lets you place *video calls*, which means you hear *and* see the other person. If either you or the person you call does not have a video camera, then Skype also enables you to place voice calls over the Internet.

Configuring Skype

Although you can sign up for a Skype account separately, this isn't necessary because Windows assigns you a Skype account automatically using your Microsoft account. This section assumes you are using a Microsoft account.

Follow these steps to configure Skype:

1. **Click Start and then click Skype.** The Find Contacts Easily screen appears.

2. **Click Continue.** The Choose Your Profile Picture screen appears.

3. **Click Upload Photo, use the Open dialog box to choose a photo, and then click Open.**

4. **Click Continue.** The Test Your Audio screen appears.

5. **Speak normally into your PC's microphone.** Skype automatically adjusts the microphone volume as you speak.

6. **Click Continue.** Skype displays your PC's camera feed.

7. **Click Continue.** Skype completes the configuration and displays its main window.

Calling someone using Skype

Once you have Skype set up on your PC, as described in the previous section, you're ready to make and accept video calls. When you make a call, note that the other person has to accept the call before the conversation can begin.

Here are the steps to follow to initiate a Skype call:

1. **Click the Calls tab.**

2. **Click + Call.** The New Call window appears.

Note

To call someone who's not in your Skype contacts list, open the New Call window and then click Dial Pad. In the dial pad that appears, enter the phone number of the person you want to call, and then click Call.

3. **Click the radio button for each contact you want to call.** Figure 5.5 shows the New Call window with one contact selected.

4. **Click Call.** Skype calls your selected contacts.

Dealing with an incoming Skype call

When someone calls your PC, you can either accept or decline the incoming call. This means you don't have to answer a call if you're too busy or otherwise occupied. When Skype detects an incoming call, you see the bar shown in Figure 5.6. You have three choices:

×	New Call	Call

Search ⋮ Dial pad

David

David McHarper

Echo / Sound Test Service

5.5 Use the New Call window to choose the contact or contacts you want to call.

- Click Video to accept the incoming connection as a video call.

- Click Audio to accept the incoming connection as a voice-only call.

- Click Decline to reject the incoming call.

5.6 Use this bar to accept or reject an incoming Skype call.

Working with Maps

Maps is an app that displays digital maps that you can use to view just about any location by searching for an address or place name. You can also use Maps to get directions to a location from any starting point.

Giving Maps access to your location

When you first start the Maps app, Windows asks if Maps is allowed to access your precise location, as shown in Figure 5.7. This means that Maps wants to access your PC's *location services*, which are background features that help determine your current location. For the best results with Maps, you should click Yes to allow Windows to give Maps access on location services.

Genius

> Maps determines your precise location using three methods. First, it looks for known Wi-Fi hotspots, which are commercial establishments that offer wireless Internet access. Second, if you're connected to the Internet, Maps uses the location information embedded in your connection's unique Internet Protocol (IP) address. Third, if your PC has a Global Positioning System (GPS) receiver, Maps uses this GPS data to pinpoint your location to within a few feet.

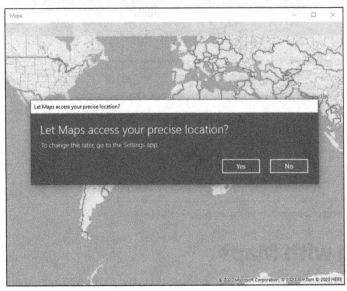

5.7 Maps asks permission to access your location when you first start the app.

If you clicked No earlier, you can reverse that decision by following these steps:

1. **In the taskbar's Search box, type** location.

2. **In the search results, click Location Privacy Settings.** The Settings app appears and displays the Location settings.

3. **If the Allow Access to Location on this Device setting is off, click Change.** Then use the dialog box that appears to click the Location Access for this Device switch to On. Click outside the dialog box to finish.

4. **Click the Allow Apps to Access Your Location switch to On.**

5. **In the Choose Which Apps Can Access Your Precise Location section, click the Maps switch to On, as shown in Figure 5.8.**

Displaying a location on a map

Here are the steps to follow to use Maps to display either your current location or a specific location:

Settings

⌂ Home

Find a setting

Privacy

Windows permissions

🔒 General

🗣 Speech

🖋 Inking & typing personalization

⚙ Diagnostics & feedback

🗂 Activity history

App permissions

📍 Location

📷 Camera

Location

Choose which apps can access your precise location

Sort by: Name ⌄

3D Viewer — Off

Camera — On
Last accessed 2/6/2020 2:41:07 PM

Desktop App Web Viewer — Off

Mail and Calendar — On
Last accessed 7/17/2020 8:51:57 AM

Maps — On
Last accessed 3/6/2020 1:14:27 PM

Skype — On
Last accessed 7/24/2020 11:47:33 AM

Weather — Off

5.8 With location services turned on, make sure Maps can access your precise location.

1. **Open the Start menu.**

2. **Click Maps.** The Maps window appears.

3. **Specify the location you want to see on the map:**

   - To show your current location, click the Show My Location icon pointed out in Figure 5.9. You can also press Ctrl+Home.

   - To show another location, use the Search box. Either type the location address and press Enter, or start typing the location name and then click the location when it appears in the search results.

Maps displays the location on the map and displays an information pane for the location, as shown in Figure 5.10.

Note

To see more map detail, either click the Zoom In icon, pointed out in Figure 5.10, or press Ctrl++ (plus); to see less map detail, either click the Zoom Out icon, pointed out in Figure 5.10, or press Ctrl+– (minus).

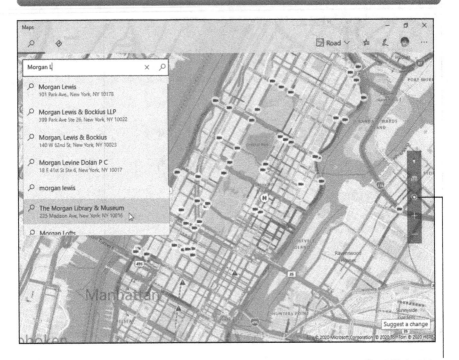

Show My Location

5.9 You can either display your current location or search for the location you want.

Getting directions to a location

Besides displaying locations, Maps also recognizes the roads and highways found in most cities, states, and countries. This means that you can use the Maps app to get specific directions for traveling from one location to another. You specify a starting point and destination for a trip, and Maps then provides you with directions for getting from one point to the other. Maps highlights the trip route on a digital map and also gives you specific details for negotiating each leg of the trip.

Directions

This icon pinpoints the location on the map

Zoom Out

Zoom In

5.10 When you choose a location, Maps shows the location on the map and displays information about the location.

Follow these steps to get directions to a location:

1. **In the Maps app, click the Directions icon.** I point out this icon in Figure 5.10. If you have the information pane for a location already displayed, you can click Directions in the information pane. Either way, Maps prompts you for your travel method and starting point, as shown in Figure 5.11.

2. **Click the travel method you'll be using: Driving, Transit, or Walking.**

3. Choose your starting point:

- To use your current location, click the My Location radio button.

- To use one of Maps' suggested starting points, click the location in the list that appears.

- To specify another starting point, use the Starting Point text box to enter the name or address of the location.

4. Type the name or address of your destination.

5. Click Get Directions. Maps displays overviews of the available routes, as shown in Figure 5.12. Note that Maps warns you if traffic is bad on a route (see the "Heavy traffic" warnings in the routes shown in Figure 5.12).

Transit

Driving   Walking

5.11 Choose a travel method and starting point.

Map Views

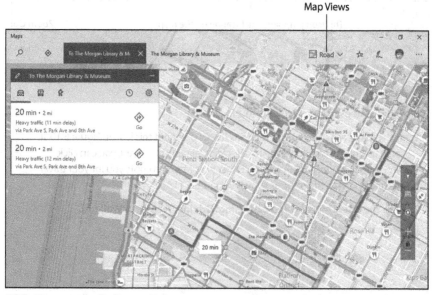

5.12 Maps usually displays multiple routes you can take to your destination.

6. **Click Go to choose the route you want to take.** Maps zooms in on the route and displays the instructions for the route.

Genius

> To see more traffic information, click Map Views (pointed out in Figure 5.12) and then click the Traffic switch to On to see the current traffic conditions on the map: Green means traffic is moving normally on that route; yellow means traffic is slower than normal; orange tells you that traffic is slow; and red means traffic is heavy.

Checking the Weather

You can use the Weather app to view your city's current conditions and five-day forecast. The Weather app takes advantage of several online weather resources to obtain up-to-the-minute conditions and forecasts.

Checking your weather forecast

The Weather app can check the forecast for a default location that you specify, or for your current location, which uses Windows location services to determine your location and display the forecast.

Creating a default location

When you first start the Weather app, follow these steps to set up your weather defaults:

1. **Click Start and then click Weather.** The Weather app appears. The first time you start the app, it asks you to specify a default temperature unit and location, as shown in Figure 5.13.

2. **Choose Fahrenheit or Celsius.**

3. **Specify your default location:**

   - If you want to use your current location as the default, choose Detect My Location.

   - To specify another location as the default, begin typing the name of the location in the Search box and then click the location when it appears in the search results.

4. **Click Start.** Weather displays the location's current conditions and forecast.

5.13 When you first launch Weather, choose a default temperature unit and location.

Changing the launch location

The default location you specified is also called the *launch location* because the conditions and forecast for that location appear each time you start the Weather app. If you need to specify a different launch location, follow these steps:

1. **In the Weather app, click Settings (pointed out in Figure 5.14).** The Settings window appears with the General tab displayed, as shown in Figure 5.14.

2. **Specify your new launch location:**

   - If you want to use your current location as the default, choose Always Detect My Location. If you see a dialog box warning you that location services are turned off for Weather, click Settings and then click the Weather switch to On.

   - To specify another location as the default, choose Default Location and then begin typing the name of the location in the Search box. Click the location when it appears in the search results.

3. **Shut down and restart Weather to put your new location into effect.**

Favorites

Settings

5.14 You can use Weather's Settings window to change your launch location.

Checking another city's weather forecast

If you're going to be traveling to another city or if you are simply curious about the weather conditions elsewhere, you can use Weather to look up the weather forecast for most cities around the world. Here are the steps to follow:

1. **In the Weather app, click Favorites (pointed out earlier in Figure 5.14).** The Favorites screen appears.

2. **Click Add (+).** The Add to Favorites screen appears.

3. **Type the name of the city you want to view.** As you type, Weather displays place names that match.

4. **When you see the location that you want, click it.** Weather adds the location to the Favorites screen.

5. **Click the location.** Weather displays the city's current conditions and forecast.

How Do I Max Out the Windows Image Tools?

Whether you load your images from a digital camera or a scanner, download them from the Internet, or draw them yourself, Windows comes with a number of useful tools for working with those images. In this chapter, you learn how to import images from a camera, scan images, and take a photo from your PC's camera. You also learn how to navigate and view your images, enhance images, fix photo problems, delete images, and much more.

Getting Images into Your PC **98**

Viewing Your Images **103**

Enhancing Your Images..................................... **107**

Repairing Your Images **111**

Getting Images into Your PC

When you get a new PC, it comes with very few, if any, images. If you have an artistic bent, you can create your own images from scratch using an app such as Paint 3D (which comes with Windows) or Adobe Illustrator (which doesn't). However, most people populate their PCs with images by importing them from a digital camera, scanning them, or by taking pictures with the PC's built-in or attached camera. The next few sections take you through these techniques.

Importing images from a smartphone or digital camera

You can import photos from a smartphone or digital camera and save them on your PC. If your camera stores the photos on a memory card, you can also use a memory card reader attached to your PC to upload the digital photos from the removable drive that Windows sets up when you insert the card. After you have the digital photos on your system, you can view or print the images.

To perform the import directly from your device, you need to connect the device to your PC in one of the following ways:

- For most smartphones and digital cameras, use a USB cable to connect your device to your PC.

- If your photos reside on a memory card and your PC has a compatible port, insert the memory card into that port.

- If your photos reside on a memory card, but your PC doesn't have a compatible port, you need to insert the memory card into a card reader and then connect that reader to your PC using a USB cable.

Here are the steps to follow to import images from a smartphone, digital camera, or memory card:

1. **Connect your device to your PC and, if applicable, make sure the device is turned on and unlocked.** If you see a message on your device asking you to give permission to your PC to access the device's photos, be sure to click or tap Allow.

2. **Click Start and then click Photos.** The Photos app appears.

3. **Click Import and then click From a USB Device.** Photos looks for connected devices and then displays the Choose a Device to Import From dialog box, shown in Figure 6.1.

4. **Click the device that has the images you want to import.** Photos opens the Import Items dialog box.

5. **Choose the images you want to import:**

   • **All images.** Use the Select list to choose All Items.

Choose a device to import from

If you don't see your device listed, make sure it's connected to your PC, turned on, and unlocked.

CF CARD
USB 2 HS-CF

EOS_DIGITAL
PCIE Card Reader

Apple iPhone
Apple iPhone

Cancel

6.1 Use this dialog box to choose the device from which you want to import your images.

   • **Images added since the last time you imported from this device.** Use the Select list to choose Items Since Last Import.

   • **Images from an entire month.** Click the check box beside the month.

   • **Individual images.** Click the check box that appears in the upper-right corner of each image, as shown in Figure 6.2.

Genius

By default, Photos groups your imported images by the month in which they were created (that is, Photos creates a subfolder in the Pictures folder for each month). To change this, click Import Settings, click either By Date (to group the images by the date they were created) or By Year (to group the images by the year they were created), and then click Done.

6. **Click Import X of Y Items, where X is the number of images you chose and Y is the total number of images on the device.** Photos imports the images and then displays them in the app.

Scanning an image

You can create a digital copy of a photo or other image by using a document scanner, or the scanner component of an all-in-one printer. The scanner copies the image to your computer, where you can then store it as a file on your hard drive. You can use a scanned image in many ways. For example, you can scan a photo to email to friends or publish on a web page. You can also scan a logo or other image to use in a document.

Import items

Select:

Custom

10 of 184 items selected

August 2020

Why don't I see all of my files?   Import 10 of 184 items   Cancel

6.2 You can choose images individually by clicking their check boxes.

Here are the steps to follow to scan an image to your PC:

1. **Turn on your scanner or all-in-one printer and position a photo or other image on the scanner bed.**

2. **In the taskbar's Search box, type** scan.

3. **Click Windows Fax and Scan.** The Windows Fax and Scan window appears.

4. **Click the Scan tab.**

5. **Click New Scan.** The New Scan dialog box appears.

6. **Use the Source list to choose from where in the device the document will be scanned.**

7. **Use the File Type list to choose the file format you want to use for the scanned image file.**

8. **Use the Resolution spin box to specify the scan resolution.** The higher the resolution, the sharper the image, but the larger the resulting file.

9. **Click Preview.** A preview of the scan appears, as shown in Figure 6.3.

New Scan   ×

Scanner: Brother DCP-L2540DW serie...   Change...

Profile: Photo (Default)   ∨

Source: Flatbed   ∨

Paper size:

Color format: Color   ∨

File type: JPG (JPG File)   ∨

Resolution (DPI): 300   ⬍

Brightness: ━━━━●━━━━ 0

Contrast: ━━━━●━━━━ 0

☐ Preview or scan images as separate files

                                    Preview   Scan   Cancel

6.3 Click Preview to see a preview of the scan, then adjust the rectangle to set the scan area.

10. **Click and drag the square handles at the corners of the rectangle to set the scan area.**

11. **Click Scan.** Windows Fax and Scan scans the image to your PC.

Genius

You can also scan an image directly into the Paint app. Start Paint by typing **paint** in the taskbar's Search box and then clicking Paint in the search results. In the Paint window, click File and then click From Scanner or Camera.

Taking a picture or video with your PC camera

If your PC comes with a built-in camera or if you have an external camera attached to your PC, you can use the camera to take a picture of yourself, someone else, your surroundings—anything you want—using the Camera app. The Camera app also gives you the option of recording a video. Either way, the Camera app stores each photo or video in a subfolder called *Camera Roll*, which appears in your Pictures folder.

Follow these steps to take a picture using the Camera app:

1. **Click Start and then click Camera.** The first time you start the Camera app, it asks for permission to use your location, so be sure to click Yes. The Camera app loads and displays a live feed from the camera.

2. **To set the photo or video quality, click Settings (the gear icon) and then use one of the following lists to choose the quality you want:**

   - **Photo quality.** Choose the number of megapixels (MP) and the aspect ratio you want in your photo. The higher the MP value, the higher the photo quality and the larger the photo file size.

   - **Video quality.** Choose the horizontal resolution (such as 720p), aspect ratio (such as 16:9), and frame rate in frames per second (such as 30fps). The higher the resolution and the higher the frame rate, the higher the video quality and the larger the video file size.

Note

The *aspect ratio* is the ratio of vertical pixels to horizontal pixels. So, video shot at 720p with an aspect ratio of 16:9 means that each frame is 1280x720. By the way, the *p* in horizontal resolution values such as 720p and 540p stands for *progressive scanning*, which means each horizontal line in a frame is drawn in sequence (as opposed to *interlaced scanning*, which draws odd-numbered lines first, then even-numbered lines).

3. **Switch to the mode you want by clicking one of the following buttons:**

   - **Photo.** Click this button if you want to capture a photo.

   - **Video.** Click this button if you want to record a video.

4. **Click one of the following buttons:**

   - If you're in photo mode, click Take Photo. Camera captures a photo.

   - If you're in video mode, click Take Video. Camera starts recording a video.

5. **If you're recording a video, click Stop Taking Video when you're finished.** The Camera app saves your video.

Viewing Your Images

Before you can work with your images, you need to view them on your PC. You do that by using either File Explorer or the Photos app to open the Pictures folder, which is a special folder designed specifically for storing images.

Using File Explorer to view your images

To get more out of the Pictures folder, you need to know not only how to open it, but also the basic techniques for opening any media folders that you have stored in the folder. Here are the basic steps:

1. **Open File Explorer.** You can either click the taskbar's pinned File Explorer icon or click Start and then click Pictures. The File Explorer program window appears.

2. **In the Quick Access list on the left, click Pictures.** The Pictures folder appears. If the image or images you want to view reside in the Pictures folder, skip to Step 5.

3. **Double-click a subfolder.** File Explorer displays the subfolder's images.

4. **Repeat Step 3 until you open the subfolder that contains the image or images you want to view.**

5. **Click an image file.** File Explorer displays the Picture Tools tab, which you can click to display the tools shown in Figure 6.4.

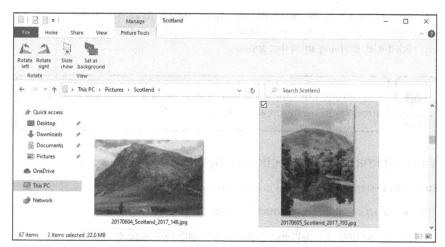

6.4 Click an image file to display the Picture Tools tab.

Genius

To use a photo as your desktop background, click the photo, click the Picture Tools tab, and then choose Set as Background.

Using the Photos app to view your images

If you want to look at several images, Windows gives you two methods to navigate backward and forward through the images in the Pictures folder. First, you can use File Explorer to open an individual image for viewing in the Photos app, and then navigate through the other images in the same folder. Second, you can use the Photos app directly to view your images by collection or by album.

Viewing individual images

Here are the steps to follow to view individual images in the Photos app:

1. **In File Explorer, open the folder that contains the images you want to view.**

2. **Double-click the first image that you want to view.** The image appears in the Photos app.

3. **To scroll right to the next image, move the mouse pointer to the right side of the window and then click the right-pointing arrow that appears (see Figure 6.5).** The Photos app displays the next image from the album.

4. **Repeat Step 3 to continue viewing the album images.** To scroll left to the previous image, move the mouse pointer to the left side of the window and then click the left-pointing arrow that appears.

Note

You can also press the Right arrow key to see the next image and the Left arrow key to see the previous image.

Viewing images by collection or by album

Follow these steps to view images in Photos by collection or by album:

1. **Click Start and then click Photos.** The Photos app appears.

2. **Click Collection.** Alternatively, you can click Albums to view your pictures by album.

See More

Photos - 20170604_Scotland_2017_148.jpg

See all photos + Add to

Move the mouse to the right edge to see the arrow

6.5 Open an image in Photos and then click the right-pointing arrow to view the next image.

Genius

Photos has no albums at first. To create an album, click New Album, click Album, choose the photos you want to include, and then click Create. To give the new album a snappy title, click the pencil icon that appears beside the default name (which is "Album").

3. **Scroll down and up to view your images by collection or album.**

4. **To get a closer look at an image, scroll to the image you want to view and then click it.** You can then navigate the images as I describe earlier. To return to the collection or album, click Back.

Starting a slide show

Instead of viewing your photos one at a time, you can easily view multiple photos by running them in a slide show. You can run the slide show from within the Photos app. The slide show displays each photo for a few seconds and then automatically moves on to the next photo. Alternatively, you can view a slide show of images using the Photos tile on the Start menu. This slide show uses recent images from your Pictures folder.

Running the slide show in the Photos app

Follow these steps to run a slide show from within the Photos app:

1. **In the Photos app, display the collection or album that contains the photos you want to display in your slide show.**

2. **Click the first image you want to display in the slide show.** Photos opens the image.

3. **Click See More (the three dots pointed out in Figure 6.5) and then click Slideshow.** You can also start the slide show by pressing F5. The Photos app begins the slide show.

Genius
You can also start a slide show using File Explorer. Navigate to the folder that contains the images you want to view, click the Picture Tools tab, and then click Slideshow. To control the playback speed, right-click the screen to display the shortcut menu, and then click the speed that you want: Slow, Medium, or Fast.

Running the slide show on the Photos tile

Follow these steps to set up a slide show on the Start menu's Photos tile:

1. **In the main Photos app window, click See More (the three dots pointed out in Figure 6.5).**

2. **Click Settings.** The Settings window appears.

3. **In the Appearance section, use the The App Tile Shows list to choose Recent Photos.** The next time that you display the Start screen, the Photos tile displays a slide show of recent images from your Pictures folder.

Note If the Photos tile doesn't show the images, right-click the tile, click More, and then click Turn Live Tile On.

Enhancing Your Images

You can use Photos to improve the look of digital photos and other images. When you open an image in Photos, the toolbar offers icons for, among other tasks, rotating and cropping the image. There's also an Edit & Create list that includes an Edit command. That command offers a number of tools to enhance the image, including cropping, rotating, and applying filters and a vignette effect. Figure 6.6 points out the available toolbar commands.

Delete Crop Edit & Create Print

Zoom Rotate Search Share

Photos - 20170605_Scotland_2017_195.jpg   — ◻ ✕

＋ Add to   🔍 🗑 ↻ 🔲 ◉ ✄ ⌄ ↪ 🖨 …

6.6 The toolbar commands you see when you open an image in the Photos app.

Cropping an image

If you have an image containing elements that you do not want or need to see, you can often cut out those elements. This is called *cropping*, and you can do this with Photos. When you crop a photo, you specify a rectangular area of the photo that you want to keep. Photos discards everything outside the rectangle.

Cropping is a useful skill to have because it can help give focus to the true subject of a photo. Cropping is also useful for removing extraneous elements that appear on or near the edges of a photo.

Follow these steps to crop an image:

1. **In Photos, display the image you want to crop.**

2. **Click Crop.** Photos displays the image editing tools and selects the Crop & Rotate tab. Photos displays a cropping rectangle on the photo.

3. **Click and drag any edge or any corner of the rectangle to define the area you want to keep, as shown in Figure 6.7.** Remember that Photos keeps the area inside the rectangle.

107

More Options

6.7 Adjust the size of the rectangle to specify the area of the image you want to keep.

Genius

Photos also enables you to crop the image using a specific aspect ratio. Common aspect ratios include square (same width and height), widescreen (16:9), and 3:2. Use the Aspect Ratio list to choose the ratio you want to use, such as Widescreen, 3:2, or 7:5. You can then click and drag the image so that the area you want to keep fits within the rectangle.

4. **Click More Options (pointed out in Figure 6.7) and then click Save.** If you prefer to leave the original as is, you can click Save a Copy, instead. Photos saves your changes.

Applying a filter

You can enhance the look of a photo by applying a filter. Some filters lighten the photo's colors to make the image stand out more, while other filters darken the image to create a moodier look. There are also several black-and-white filters you can apply.

Here are the steps to follow to apply a filter to an image:

1. **In Photos, display the image you want to work with.**

2. **Click Edit & Create (pointed out earlier in Figure 6.6) and then click Edit.** Photos displays the image editing tools.

3. **Click Filters.** Photos displays the Filter pane, as shown in Figure 6.8.

6.8 Use the Filter pane to apply and adjust a filter.

4. **Click the filter you want to apply.**

5. **Click and drag the Filter Intensity slider to set the intensity of the filter.**

6. **Click More Options (pointed out earlier in Figure 6.7) and then click Save.** If you prefer to leave the original as is, you can click Save a Copy, instead. Photos saves your changes.

Adding a vignette effect

The vignette effect darkens the edges and corners of the photo, which adds a natural frame around the image and draws attention to the interior of the photo.

Here are the steps to follow to apply a vignette effect to an image:

1. **In Photos, display the image you want to work with.**

2. **Click Edit & Create (pointed out earlier in Figure 6.6) and then click Edit.** Photos displays the image editing tools.

3. **Click Adjustments.**

4. **Click and drag the Vignette slider until you get the vignette effect the way you want it (see Figure 6.9).**

6.9 Drag the Vignette slider to apply a vignette effect to your image.

5. **Click More Options (pointed out earlier in Figure 6.7) and then click Save.** If you prefer to leave the original as is, you can click Save a Copy, instead. Photos saves your changes.

Repairing Your Images

Unless you're a professional photographer (and even if you are), it's a rare photo that doesn't have some sort of error, however minor. The image could be over- or under-exposed, the colors might look off, one or more of your subjects might have red eye, or an otherwise-perfect image might have a slight flaw. Fortunately, Photos offers tools to repair these and other image glitches.

Rotating an image

Depending on how you hold your camera when you take a shot, the resulting photo might show the subject sideways or upside down. To fix this problem, you can use Photos to rotate the photo so that the subject appears right side up.

Here are the steps to follow to rotate an image:

1. **In Photos, display the image you want to work with.**

2. **Click Edit & Create (pointed out earlier in Figure 6.6) and then click Edit.** Photos displays the image editing tools with the Crop & Rotate tab selected.

3. **Click Rotate until the image is the way you want it.** You can also rotate the image by pressing Ctrl+R. If you want a mirror image of the photo, instead, click Flip to flip the image horizontally.

4. **Click More Options (pointed out earlier in Figure 6.7) and then click Save.** If you prefer to leave the original as is, you can click Save a Copy, instead. Photos saves your changes.

Genius

You can also rotate an image using File Explorer. Navigate to and click the image, click the Picture Tools tab, and then click either Rotate Left or Rotate Right until the image has the orientation you want.

Straightening an image

If you didn't hold your camera level when you took the shot, your photo will appear tilted to the left or right. In many photos this tilt isn't noticeable, but if your photo has strong or prominent horizontal lines, the tilt will detract from your image. To fix this, you can straighten the image.

Here are the steps to follow to straighten an image:

1. **In Photos, display the image you want to work with.**

2. **Click Edit & Create (pointed out earlier in Figure 6.6) and then click Edit.** Photos displays the image editing tools with the Crop & Rotate tab selected.

3. **Click and drag the Straightening slider left or right until your image is straight.**

4. **Click More Options (pointed out earlier in Figure 6.7) and then click Save.** If you prefer to leave the original as is, you can click Save a Copy, instead. Photos saves your changes.

Adjusting the light

Even if you take quite a bit of care setting up and taking your shot, you might still end up with a photo that is under- or overexposed, has shadows that are too dark or too light, or has poor overall contrast. If the lighting in a photo is off, the Photos app offers the following sliders that you can use to make adjustments:

- **Contrast.** Use this slider to adjust the distribution of the photo's tones. If the tones in your photo are starkly different, lower the contrast to make them more alike; if your photo is bland because the tones are all alike, increase the contrast to make the tones stand out.

- **Exposure.** Use this slider to set the overall lighting of the photo. If your entire photo is washed out because it's too light, decrease the exposure to get a darker image; if your entire photo is muddy because it's too dark, increase the exposure to get a lighter image.

- **Highlights.** Use this slider to adjust how intense the brightest parts of the image appear. If your photo has one or more areas that are washed out because they're too bright, reduce the Highlights value to counter that effect.

- **Shadows.** Use this slider to adjust how intense the darkest parts of the image appear. If your photo has one or more areas that show no detail because they're too dark, reduce the Shadows value to try and bring back some of that detail.

Here are the steps to follow to adjust the light of an image:

1. **In Photos, display the image you want to work with.**

2. **Click Edit & Create (pointed out earlier in Figure 6.6) and then click Edit.** Photos displays the image editing tools.

3. **Click Adjustments.** Photos displays the Adjustments pane.

4. **Click Light.** Photos displays the light-related sliders, as shown in Figure 6.10.

If you make a mess of your image, click Reset to undo all your lighting changes

6.10 Use the Light sliders—Contrast, Exposure, Highlights, and Shadows—to adjust the lighting of your image.

5. **Use the four Light sliders—Contrast, Exposure, Highlights, and Shadows—to adjust the image lighting as needed.**

6. **Click More Options (pointed out earlier in Figure 6.7) and then click Save.** If you prefer to leave the original as is, you can click Save a Copy, instead. Photos saves your changes.

Adjusting the colors

If the colors in a photo or other image look off, Photos offers two sliders that you can use to make adjustments:

⦿ **Tint.** Use this slider to add more green or magenta to an image's colors to solve colorcast problems (where the colors of some objects are off because they reflect nearby colors, such as grass).

⦿ **Warmth.** Use this slider to adjust the color *temperature*, which refers to the relative warmth of the colors, where cooler means bluer and hotter means redder.

Here are the steps to follow to adjust the color of an image:

1. **In Photos, display the image you want to work with.**

2. **Click Edit & Create (pointed out earlier in Figure 6.6) and then click Edit.** Photos displays the image editing tools.

3. **Click Adjustments.** Photos displays the Adjustments pane.

4. **Click Color.** Photos displays the color-related sliders, as shown in Figure 6.11.

6.11 Use the Color sliders—Tint and Warmth—to adjust the colors of your image.

114

5. **Use the two Color sliders—Tint and Warmth—to adjust the image colors as needed.**

6. **Click More Options (pointed out earlier in Figure 6.7) and then click Save.** If you prefer to leave the original as is, you can click Save a Copy, instead. Photos saves your changes.

Enhancing image clarity

The *clarity* of an image reflects how sharp or blurry the edges within the image appear:

- The higher the clarity value, the sharper the image. This is generally what you want, but cranking up the clarity *too* high can make the image look artificial and processed.

- The lower the clarity value, the blurrier the image. This can be useful for certain artistic effects, but going too low can make your image look muddy and undefined.

Follow these steps to adjust the clarity of an image:

1. **In Photos, display the image you want to work with.**

2. **Click Edit & Create (pointed out earlier in Figure 6.6) and then click Edit.** Photos displays the image editing tools.

3. **Click Adjustments.** Photos displays the Adjustments pane.

4. **Use the Clarity slider to adjust the image clarity as needed.**

5. **Click More Options (pointed out earlier in Figure 6.7) and then click Save.** If you prefer to leave the original as is, you can click Save a Copy, instead. Photos saves your changes.

Getting rid of red eye

When you use a flash to take a picture of one or more people, in some cases the flash may reflect off the subjects' retinas. The result is the common phenomenon of *red eye*, where each pupil appears red instead of black. If you have a photo where one or more subjects have red eyes due to the camera flash, you can use Photos to remove the red eye and give your subjects a more natural look.

Follow these steps to get rid of red eye in an image:

1. **In Photos, display the image you want to work with.**

2. **Click Edit & Create (pointed out earlier in Figure 6.6) and then click Edit.** Photos displays the image editing tools.

3. **Click Adjustments.** Photos displays the Adjustments pane.

4. **Click Red Eye.** Photos adds a blue circle to the mouse pointer.

5. **Position the blue circle over a red eye and click.** Photos removes the red eye.

6. **Repeat Step 5 as often as needed to remove all of the red eye from the image.**

7. **Click More Options (pointed out earlier in Figure 6.7) and then click Save.** If you prefer to leave the original as is, you can click Save a Copy, instead. Photos saves your changes.

Fixing small flaws

If an otherwise-perfect image has a small flaw or blemish—for example, a speck of dirt on the subject of a portrait or a plane that wandered into a landscape shot—you might be able to remove that flaw using the Spot Fix tool. Spot Fix works by replacing the pixels of the flawed portion of the image with pixels from the area that surrounds the flaw. Ideally, these replaced pixels will leave you with a seamless (and flawless) image and no one will be the wiser.

Follow these steps to wield the Spot Fix tool:

1. **In Photos, display the image you want to work with.**

2. **Click Edit & Create (pointed out earlier in Figure 6.6) and then click Edit.** Photos displays the image editing tools.

3. **Click Adjustments.** Photos displays the Adjustments pane.

4. **Click Spot Fix.** Photos adds a blue circle to the mouse pointer.

5. **Position the blue circle over the image flaw and click.** Photos removes the portion of the flaw that lies within the circle.

6. **Repeat Step 5 as often as needed either to fix a single flaw or to fix any other flaws in the image.**

7. **Click More Options (pointed out earlier in Figure 6.7) and then click Save.** If you prefer to leave the original as is, you can click Save a Copy, instead. Photos saves your changes.

Can I Share My Computer?

Network access

Choose people to share with

Type a name and then click Add, or click the arrow to find someone.

Name	Permission Level
Greg	Read ▼
Paul McFedries (paulmcfedries@hotmail.com)	Owner

✓ Read
Read/Write
Remove

I'm having trouble sharing

Share   Cancel

Do you share your computer with other people, either at work or at home? Then you've probably run into one undeniable fact: People are individuals with minds of their own! One person prefers Windows in a black-and-purple color scheme; another person just loves changing the desktop background; yet another person prefers to have a ton of shortcuts on the Windows desktop; and, of course, everybody uses a different mix of apps and creates their own documents. You can satisfy all these diverse tastes and prevent conflicts by learning a few useful tools and techniques for sharing your computer with others.

Sharing Your PC via User Accounts **120**

Sharing Your PC with a Child **127**

Sharing PC Resources **132**

Sharing Your PC via User Accounts

To accommodate multiple users on your PC, Windows enables you to set up a different *user account* for each person who uses the computer. A user account is a kind of storage area where Windows keeps track of one person's documents, email, apps, and customizations. These accounts keep your stuff separate from everyone else's stuff, including documents and programs, desktop and Start menu configuration, Edge web browser favorites, and more. This means everyone can customize Windows to their heart's content without foisting their tastes on anyone else.

Creating a user account

When you add an account for someone to use your PC, you'll most likely want that person to sign in using a Microsoft account, which gives the person access to a wider variety of features, apps, and settings that aren't available to non-Microsoft account users. The next few sections show you the various methods you can use to add a user account to your PC.

Adding a user who already has a Microsoft account

The easiest way to create a user account is for someone who already has a Microsoft account. Here are the steps to follow:

1. **In the taskbar's Search box, type** add user **and then click Add, Edit, or Remove Other Users in the search results.** The Settings app opens and displays the People on This Device tab of the Accounts settings.

2. **Click Add Someone Else to This PC.** The Microsoft Account dialog box appears.

3. **Type the user's Microsoft account email address and then click Next.** Windows creates the account.

4. **Click Finish.** The new user can now use her Microsoft account credentials to sign in to Windows, as described later in this chapter.

Adding a user by creating a new Microsoft account

If you want to add someone who doesn't yet have a Microsoft account, you need to jump through a few extra hoops to create the account. Here are the steps to follow:

1. **In the taskbar's Search box, type** add user **and then click Add, Edit, or Remove Other Users in the search results.** The Settings app opens and displays the People on This Device tab of the Accounts settings.

2. **Click Add Someone Else to This PC.** The Microsoft Account dialog box appears.

3. **Click I Don't Have This Person's Sign-In Information.** The Create Account dialog box appears.

4. **Type the new user's email address and then click Next.** Windows prompts you for a password.

Genius

If the new user doesn't have an email address, click Get a New Email Address in the Create Account dialog box, type a username, choose either outlook. com or hotmail.com as the domain, and then click Next. Enter a password, click Next, and then resume this procedure with Step 6.

5. **Type a password for the user's new Microsoft account and then click Next.**

6. **Type the user's first name and last name, then click Next.**

7. **Choose the user's country, enter the user's date of birth, and then click Next.** The Verify Email dialog box appears and Microsoft sends a confirmation email to the address you specified in Step 4.

8. **Access the user's email, open the confirmation email, and locate the security code.**

9. **In the Verify Email dialog box, enter the security code and click Next.**

10. **Type the name you want to use for the new account.**

11. **Type a password and then retype the password for the new account.**

12. **For each security question, use the list to choose the question you want to use and then enter an answer for each question.**

13. **Click Next.** The new user can now use her Microsoft account credentials to sign in to Windows, as described later in this chapter.

Adding a user without a Microsoft account

If you'd rather add a user to your PC without that user being tied to a Microsoft account—that is, if you want to create a so-called *local account*—here are the steps to follow:

Caution

The steps in this section were accurate as this book went to press. However, there were also rumors floating around that one day—perhaps even one day soon—Microsoft will do away with the option to create local accounts. It's clear Microsoft would prefer all users to have Microsoft accounts, so be forewarned that the steps that follow might not be available by the time you read this.

1. **In the taskbar's Search box, type** add user **and then click Add, Edit, or Remove Other Users in the search results.** The Settings app opens and displays the People on This Device tab of the Accounts settings.

2. **Click Add Someone Else to This PC.** The Microsoft Account dialog box appears.

3. **Click I Don't Have This Person's Sign-In Information.** The Create Account dialog box appears.

4. **Click Add a User Without a Microsoft account.** The Create an Account for This PC screen appears.

5. **Type the name you want to use for the new account.**

6. **Type the password and then retype a password for the new account.**

7. **For each security question, use the list to choose the question you want to use and then enter an answer for each question.**

8. **Click Next.** The new user can now use her Microsoft account credentials to sign in to Windows, as described next.

Genius

If you decide later that you want the local account to be a Microsoft account instead, sign in to the account, click Start, click the tile for the user, and then click Change Account Settings. In the Your Info screen that appears, click Sign in with a Microsoft Account Instead and follow the screens that appear.

Switching between accounts

Windows also supports a feature called *fast user switching*; what this means is that different users can switch in and out of Windows but leave their programs running. For example, suppose little Alice is battling some aliens and Dad needs to check his email. In the old days, Alice would have to shut down her game so that Dad could log on and run his email app. In Windows, Alice can leave her game running while Dad switches to his account and does his email duties. Alice can then switch back right away and resume her game.

Switching between accounts when Windows is running

Here are the steps to follow to switch from one user account to another while Windows is running:

1. **Click Start and then click the tile for the current user.** Windows displays a list of the user accounts on the PC, as shown in Figure 7.1.

Other users on this PC

= **START**   Productivity

                                      Office   S   Mail

P₀ Change account settings
A   Lock
[→ Sign out   Calendar   Alarms & Clock   Calculator

    Paul M   Play
    Signed in
R   Alice

R   Greg
                                      Xbox Console...   Xbox Game Bar

    Paul McFedries
                                      Solitaire   Mixed Reality...
D   Documents
                                      Explore
⊠   Pictures

⚙   Settings

⏻   Power   Microsoft Store   Microsoft Edge

⊞   ⌕ Type here to search   O   ⊟   C

Current user's tile

7.1 On the Start menu, click the current user's tile to see a list of the PC's user accounts.

2. Click the user account you want to switch to. Windows opens the sign-in screen and prompts you for the user account PIN or password.

3. Type the PIN or password.

4. Press Enter or click Submit. The first time you switch to a new account, Windows takes a few moments to configure the account.

Switching between accounts at startup

Another way to switch to another user account on your PC is to choose the account at startup using either of the following techniques:

◉ Start or restart your PC.

◉ Click Start, click the tile for the current user, and then click Sign Out.

Either way, you end up at the Lock screen. Press Enter to bring up the sign-in screen, which will look similar to the one shown in Figure 7.2. A list of the user accounts on the PC appears on the left. Click a user and then enter that user's PIN or password to switch to that account.

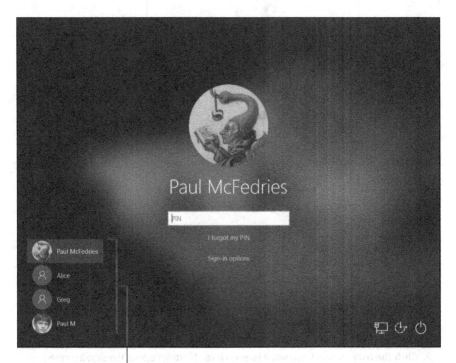

User accounts on this PC

7.2 Boot your PC or sign out of the current user to get to the sign-in screen, which contains a list of the PC's user accounts.

Handling a Forgotten Password

When you set up your password as described earlier, Windows asks you to type answers to several security questions. If you can't remember your password, you need to supply the answers to those questions before you can create a new password. To reset your password, follow these steps:

1. **In the sign-in screen, leave the password text box blank.**

2. **Click Submit or press Enter.** Windows tells you the password is incorrect.

3. **Click OK to return to the sign-in screen.**

4. **Click Reset Password to display your security questions.**

5. **Answer the questions.**

6. **Click Submit or press Enter.**

7. **Enter your new password.**

Changing your user account picture

When you create a user account, Windows assigns it a default picture, which appears in the user's Start screen tile, the Accounts screen of the Settings app, and the sign-in screen. Unfortunately, this default picture is a generic silhouette of a person's head and upper torso, so it's not very interesting or useful. If you have a more suitable picture that you would prefer to use, you can change your picture. You can either use an existing image or you can take a photo using your PC's camera.

Choosing an image file to use as your account picture

You can use an existing image as your user account picture by following these steps:

1. **Click Start and then click the tile for the current user.**

2. **Click Change Account Settings.** The Settings app appears with the Your Info tab displayed.

3. **In the Create Your Picture section, click Browse For One.** The Open dialog box appears.

4. **Click the picture you want to use and then click Choose Picture.** Settings returns you to the Your Info tab and displays the new picture.

Taking a photo to use as your account picture

If your PC has a camera, you can take a photo to use as your user account picture by following these steps:

1. **Click Start and then click the tile for the current user.**

2. **Click Change Account Settings.** The Settings app appears with the Your Info tab displayed.

3. **In the Create Your Picture section, click Camera.** The Camera app opens.

4. **Position yourself within the screen and then click Take Photo to take the picture.** The Camera app displays the photo and adds a circle that defines the area of the photo it will use for your account picture.

5. **Click and drag within the circle to position the image how you want.**

6. **Click and drag the circle's handles to set the size of the circle.**

7. **Click Done.** Settings returns you to the Your Info tab and displays the new picture.

Changing the account type

Windows offers two different user account types:

- **Administrator.** This type of account has wide (but not complete) access to the computer. An administrator can install any type of program or device; make changes that affect the entire system; and add, change, and delete user accounts. Note, however, that the administrator can't examine the private documents of any other user.

- **Standard user.** This type of account has access to only some of the computer's features. A standard user can view her own files, view those files that have been set up to be shared with other users, perform her own customizations, and change her password.

By default, Windows has only one administrator account, and that's whatever account you set up when you went through the initial Windows configuration. Every other account you create (as described earlier) is automatically a standard user.

If you have another user of your PC that you trust implicitly (such as your spouse or significant other), you can change that user to an administrator. Similarly, if you've granted administrator status to an account, you can revoke that status and revert the account to a standard user.

Either way, follow these steps:

1. **Sign in to Windows using your administrator account.**

2. **Click Start and then click the tile for your user account.**

3. **Click Change Account Settings.** The Settings app appears with the Your Info tab displayed.

4. **Click People on This Device.** Settings displays a list of your PC's user accounts.

5. **Click the user account you want to change.**

6. **Click Change Account Type.** The Change Account Type dialog box appears, as shown in Figure 7.3.

Change account type

Change account type

Alice
Local Account

Account type

Standard User

OK   Cancel

7.3 Use the Change Account Type dialog box to choose the user's new account type.

7. **Use the Account Type list to choose the type you want to apply to the user: Administrator or Standard User.**

8. **Click OK.** Windows changes the user's account type.

Deleting an account

If you have an account you no longer use, follow these steps to remove it from your PC:

1. **In the taskbar's Search box, type** add user **and then click Add, Edit, or Remove Other Users in the search results.** The Settings app opens and displays the People on This Device tab of the Accounts settings.

2. **Click the user you want to delete.**

3. **Click Remove.** Windows asks you to confirm the deletion of the account and all its data.

4. **Click Delete Account and Data. Windows deletes the account.**

Sharing Your PC with a Child

If you have a child that you want to give access to your PC, you can add that child as a family member rather than as a regular user account. The advantage is that you gain access to an extensive array of settings that enable you to restrict the child's activities, content, and screen time. The next section shows you how to add a child as a family member, then I take you through the types of restrictions you can apply.

Note

Your child must have an email account to be added as a family member.

Adding a child to your PC

Here are the steps to follow to add a child to your PC as a family member:

1. **Sign in to Windows using an administrator account.**

2. **Click Start and then click the tile for your user account.**

3. **Click Change Account Settings.** The Settings app appears with the Your Info tab displayed.

4. **Click Family & Other Users.**

5. **In the Your Family section, click Add Someone.** The Add Someone dialog box appears.

6. **Click the Create One for a Child link.** The Create Account dialog box appears.

Note

If your child already has a Microsoft account, type the child's Microsoft account email address and then click Next.

7. **Type a username, choose either outlook.com or hotmail.com as the domain, and then click Next.** The Create a Password dialog box appears.

8. **Enter a password and click Next.** The What's Your Name dialog box appears.

9. **Type the child's first name and last name, then click Next.**

10. **Choose your country, enter the child's date of birth, and then click Next.** Settings adds the child to your family group.

11. **Click Close.** Your child now appears in the Family & Other Users tab under the Your Family heading.

Setting restrictions on a child's account

When you add a child as a family member on your PC, as described in the previous section, you can use Microsoft's online family settings to enable various monitoring and restriction features. For example, you can receive weekly email reports of your child's web browsing activity, restrict the hours each day that your child is able to use the PC, and block games, apps, media, and websites that are inappropriate for a child.

Accessing the family settings online

To set restrictions on a child's account, you need to go online and follow these steps:

1. **Sign in to Windows using an administrator account.**

2. **Click Start and then click the tile for your user account.**

3. **Click Change Account Settings.** The Settings app appears with the Your Info tab displayed.

4. **Click Family & Other Users.**

5. **In the Your Family section, click Manage Family Settings Online.** The Edge browser appears.

6. **Click Sign In Now, then follow the prompts to enter your Microsoft account email address and password.** Edge displays the Family tab of your Microsoft account, as shown in Figure 7.4.

7.4 Use the Family tab of your Microsoft account to set restrictions on a child's account.

Enabling activity reporting

Once you have the Family tab displayed in Edge, follow these to enable *activity reporting*, which gives you weekly reports of a family member's online activities:

1. **In the Family tab of your Microsoft account, click the Activity link for the child you want to monitor.** Edge opens the settings for the family member and displays the Activity tab.

2. **Click the Activity Reporting switch to On.**

3. **Make sure the Email Weekly Reports to Me switch is set to On, as shown in Figure 7.5.** Microsoft will now email you weekly activity reports. Note, too, that you can also monitor your child's activities using the Activity tab.

Alice McFedries

See other family member accounts ∨

Help Alice shop within limits
Add money >

Create healthy habits
Set up limits >

Your wallet is safe
View purchase history >

Activity   Screen time   App and game limits   Content restrictions   Spending   Find your child

View activity from   August 21 - today ∨

∨ Manage

To block inappropriate websites and receive web browsing activity reports, make sure family members are using Microsoft Edge or Internet Explorer. Go to **Content restrictions** to change what type of stuff they can get, and **Screen time** to change how much time they can spend using it.

Activity reporting
On

Email weekly reports to me
On

Feedback

7.5 Use the Activity tab to enable weekly activity reporting for a child's account.

Setting screen time limits

Follow these steps to set restrictions on the times that a child can use the PC:

1. **In the Family tab of your Microsoft account, click the Screen Time link for the child you want to monitor.** Edge opens the settings for the family member and displays the Screen Time tab.

2. **Click the Windows 10 switch to On.**

3. **For a particular day, click the time you want to work with.** A window opens in which you can specify a time range that your child can use the PC (see Figure 7.6).

On Saturday, they can have screen time

From | To
1:00 PM | 5:00 PM | Add

Screen time schedule

9:00 AM | 12:00 PM | 🗑 Remove

Cancel | Save

7.6 Use this window to specify when the child can access the PC.

4. **Click the From and To times to set the time in 30-minute increments.**

5. **Click Add.** To delete a previously added schedule, you can click Remove beside the schedule.

6. **Click Save.** Windows saves the screen time limit you chose.

7. **Repeat Steps 3 to 6 to set more screen time limits as needed.**

Restricting the content your child can view

Follow these steps to restrict the apps, games, and websites a child can view:

1. **In the Family tab of your Microsoft account, click More Options and then click Content Restrictions for the child you want to monitor.** Edge opens the settings for the family member and displays the Content Restrictions tab.

2. **In the Apps, Games, and Media section, use the Allow Apps and Games Rated For list to choose the maximum rated age your child can use for apps and games.**

3. **Click the Block Inappropriate Websites switch to On.**

4. **If there's a website you definitely want the child to access, type the site address in the Add a Website You Want to Allow text box, and then click Add (+).** Repeat as needed for other sites you want to allow.

Note

If you want to be super-restrictive, click the Only Allow These Websites check box. This means that your child can only visit the sites you specify.

5. **If there's a website you definitely don't want the child to access, type the site address in the Add a Website You Want to Block text box, and then click Add (+).** Repeat as needed for other sites you want to block.

Sharing PC Resources

You can share documents and folders of your choice with other users set up on your computer. Sharing a document or folder enables you to work on a file with other people without having to send them a copy of the file.

Sharing a document or folder

You can set up each document or folder with one of the following permissions:

● **Read permission.** Users can't make changes to the document or folder.

● **Read/write permission.** Users can view and make changes to the document or folder.

Follow these steps to share a document or folder:

1. **Use File Explorer to open the folder containing the item you want to share.**

2. **Click the document or folder you want to share.**

3. **Click the Share tab.**

4. **Use the Share With list to choose specific people.** Windows launches the Sharing Wizard, which appears as the Network Access dialog box.

5. **Use the list to choose the name of the user.**

6. **Click Add.**

7. **Use the Permission Level list to choose the permission level (Read or Read/Write), as shown in Figure 7.7.**

7.7 Add a user and then choose that user's permission level.

8. **Repeat Steps 5 through 7 for each user you want to include in the share.**

9. **Click Share.** Windows shares the document or folder and then displays a Network Access dialog box like the one shown in Figure 7.8.

7.8 Windows displays this dialog box after it has shared the document or folder.

133

10. Use the links in the Network Access dialog box to send the address of the shared resource to the user (or users):

- **E-mail.** Click this link to send the address via email.

- **Copy.** Click this link to copy the address to memory. You can then open a program such as WordPad, click Edit, and then click Paste to paste the address.

11. Click Done.

Switching to advanced sharing

If your computer is part of a network, it's common to give other users access to some of your files by sharing one or more folders with the network. As I showed in the previous section, by default, Windows runs the Sharing Wizard when you opt to share a folder. The Sharing Wizard enables you to choose which users can access the folder and how each person shares it: with Read or Read/Write permission.

If you want to apply more sophisticated sharing options, such as the folder permissions discussed in the next section, you need to switch to the advanced sharing features that

Windows offers. These features enable you to set permissions for specific users and for groups of users (such as Administrators or Guests), create multiple shares for the same folder, and more.

Here are the steps to follow to turn off the Sharing Wizard and use advanced permissions instead:

1. **In the taskbar's Search box, type** file options **and then click File Explorer Options in the search results.** The File Explorer Options dialog box appears.

2. **Click the View tab.**

3. **Clear the Use Sharing Wizard check box, as shown in Figure 7.9.**

4. **Click OK.** Windows switches to its advanced sharing options.

Clear this check box

7.9 Clear the Use Sharing Wizard check box to switch to using advanced sharing options.

Sharing a folder with other users on the network

The purpose of most networks is to share resources between the computers connected to the network. For example, the users on a network can share a single printer or an Internet connection. This resource sharing also applies to documents. It might be a presentation that you want other people to comment on, a database with information that you want others to use, or a worksheet that you want people to modify. In all these cases, the easiest way to give other people access to your documents is to share the document folder with the network.

This section shows you how to set up basic folder sharing. See the next section to learn how to protect your shared folders with permissions.

Note

To follow the steps in this section, you need to deactivate the Sharing Wizard, as I describe earlier.

Follow these steps to share a folder:

1. **In File Explorer, open the folder that contains the folder you want to share and then click that folder to choose it.**

2. **Click the Share tab.**

3. **Click Advanced Sharing.** The folder's Properties dialog box appears with the Sharing tab displayed.

4. **Click Advanced Sharing.** The Advanced Sharing dialog box appears.

5. **Click the Share This Folder check box, as shown in Figure 7.10.**

6. **Edit the Share Name, if desired.**

7. **You have two choices from here:**

   - If you want to share the folder with the default permissions that Windows assigns—that is, giving everyone on your network Read permission—click OK to return the Properties dialog box and then click Close.

   - If you want to apply advanced file permissions, follow the steps in the next section.

7.10 Click the Share This Folder check box.

Genius

If you want to change the share name of your folder, first follow Steps 1 to 4 to display the Advanced Sharing dialog box. Click Add to display the New Share dialog box, type the new share name you want to use, and then click OK. Use the Share Name list to choose the old share name and then click Remove. Click OK and then click Close.

Protect your shared folders with advanced file permissions

Windows offers a sophisticated file security system called *permissions*. Permissions specify exactly what the groups or users can do with the contents of a protected folder. There are three types of permissions:

- **Full Control.** Network users can view and modify the shared resource, as well as change permissions on the resource.

- **Change.** Network users can view the folder contents, open files, edit files, create new files and subfolders, delete files, and run programs.

- **Read.** Network users can open files but can't edit them.

Genius

You can save time when setting up shared folder security by assigning permissions to groups instead of individual users. For example, if you know that some of the network users have administrator accounts, you could add the Administrators group; similarly, all standard Windows users are part of the Users group.

In each case, you can either allow the permission or deny it. Here are the steps to follow to set advanced permissions on a shared folder:

1. **If you don't already have the Advanced Sharing dialog box open for a folder, follow Steps 1 to 4 in the previous section.**

2. **From the Advanced Sharing dialog box, click Permissions.** The folder's Permissions dialog box appears.

3. **Click Add.** The Select Users or Groups dialog box appears.

4. **Type the name of the user or group you want to work with.**

Genius

If you're not sure of the correct user or group name, click Advanced to expand the dialog box, then click Find Now to display a list of all your PC's users and groups. Choose the name of the user or group you want to add and then click OK.

5. **Click OK.** The user or group appears in the Group or User Names list, as shown in Figure 7.11.

6. **Click the new user.**

7. **In the Allow column, click each permission that you want to allow.**

8. **Click OK.**

9. **Click OK in the Advanced Sharing dialog box.**

10. **Click Close in the folder's Properties dialog box.** Windows protects the folder with the permissions you selected.

Permissions for Budget ☒

Share Permissions

Group or user names:

Everyone
Greg (TABLETPC\Greg)

Add...   Remove

Permissions for Greg   Allow   Deny

Full Control   ☐   ☐
Change   ☐   ☐
Read   ☑   ☐

OK   Cancel   Apply

7.11 The name of the user or group you added appears in the folder's Permissions dialog box.

Caution

By default, Windows assigns Read permission to the Everyone group. This group represents every user or group not otherwise specified in the Permissions dialog box. For extra security, make sure you don't give the Everyone group Full Control or Change permission. If you want only your specified users and groups to access your shared folder, click Everyone, and then click Remove.

How Can I Get More from a Tablet PC?

Home

Find a setting

Devices

Bluetooth & other devices

Printers & scanners

Mouse

Touchpad

Typing

Typing

Touch keyboard

Play key sounds as I type

On

Capitalize the first letter of each sentence

On

Use all uppercase letters when I double-tap Shift

On

Show the touch keyboard when not in tablet mode and there's no keyboard attached

Off

1 q	2 w	3 e	4 r	5 t	6 y	7 u	8 i	9 o	0 p	⌫
a	s	d	f	g	h	j	k	l	'	↵
↑	z	x	c	v	b	n	m	,	.	?	↑
&123	Ctrl	☺						<	>

A *tablet PC* (also called a *touch PC*) is a computer that's designed to control Windows, use apps, and input text by touching the screen—using a finger or a digital pen—instead of using a separate keyboard and mouse. Some tablet PC's are screen-only devices, while others are so-called *2-in-1* devices that can operate as a regular notebook PC but can also collapse down to a screen-only tablet. Windows offers many options to support tablet PCs and this chapter takes you through all the features and settings that can help you get the most out of your tablet PC investment.

Working in Tablet Mode 140

Controlling Windows with Gestures 141

Inputting Text with the Touch Keyboard 143

Setting Power and Battery Options 149

Working in Tablet Mode

If you're using a touch-based PC or a tablet device, Windows will automatically reconfigure the screen into *tablet mode*, which is designed to make it easier for you to navigate and launch items using touches and other gestures. However, you might find that using this new interface is not easier at first. To get more out of this interface and to learn how to operate your tablet PC, you need to familiarize yourself with tablet mode.

Figure 8.1 shows a typical screen that Windows displays at startup when your PC is in tablet mode.

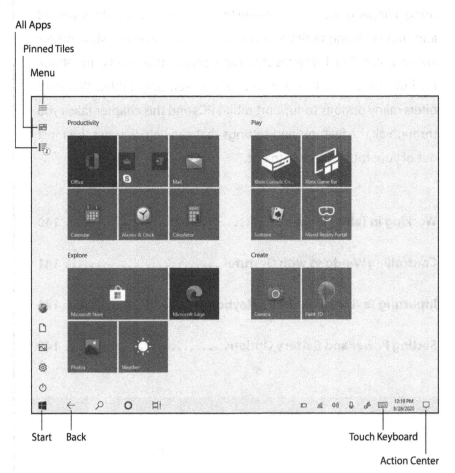

8.1 Windows in tablet mode.

Genius

By default, Windows doesn't start automatically in tablet mode if your tablet PC has a keyboard attached. To configure Windows to always start in tablet mode, open Settings, tap System, tap Tablet, and the use the When I Sign In list to choose Always Use Tablet Mode.

Here are some items to note in the tablet mode screen:

- Tablet mode automatically displays a full-screen version of the Start menu's pinned tiles.

- To see a list of all your installed apps, tap All Apps (pointed out in Figure 8.1).

- To see the Start menu command names, tap Menu (pointed out in Figure 8.1). Tap Menu again to hide the command names.

- In an app, you can tap Back (pointed out in Figure 8.1) to return to either the previous app screen or to the Start screen.

- To return directly to the Start screen, you can tap Start.

- To toggle tablet mode on and off, you can tap Action Center (pointed out in Figure 8.1) and then tap Tablet Mode (see Figure 8.2).

Tap to toggle tablet mode

8.2 In the Action Center, tap Tablet Mode to toggle tablet mode on and off.

Controlling Windows with Gestures

You can get the most out of your Windows tablet by learning the various gestures that you can use to initiate actions, manipulate data, and control the elements on your screen. Traditional computers use the mouse and keyboard to input data and make things happen. A tablet lacks these input devices; instead, you must rely on your fingers because tablets are built to respond to touches on the glass screen surface. Some tablets also come with a small pen-like device called a *stylus*, which you can use instead of your finger for some actions.

Understanding gestures

Here's a summary of the basic gestures you can use with your tablet or touch PC:

- **Tap.** Use your finger to touch the screen and then immediately release it. You use this gesture to initiate an action.

- **Double-tap.** Tap and release the screen twice, one tap right after the other. You also use this gesture to initiate an action, although mostly with older desktop programs.

- **Tap and hold.** Press your finger on the screen for a second or two. This gesture is equivalent to right-clicking with a mouse. For example, tapping and holding usually displays a menu of options related to whatever screen object you're pressing.

- **Slide.** Place your finger on the screen, move your finger, and then release. You use this gesture either to move an object from one place to another or to scroll the screen in the same direction as your finger.

- **Swipe.** Quickly and briefly run your finger along the screen. Windows has specific swipe gestures that display screen elements. For example, in the Lock screen you swipe up to display the sign-in screen.

- **Pinch.** Place two fingers (or one finger and a stylus) apart on the screen and bring them closer together. This gesture zooms out on whatever is displayed on the screen, such as a photo.

- **Spread.** Place two fingers (or one finger and a stylus) close together on the screen and move them farther apart. This gesture zooms in on whatever is displayed on the screen, such as a photo.

- **Turn.** Place two fingers (or one finger and a stylus) on the screen and turn them clockwise or counterclockwise. This gesture rotates whatever is displayed on the screen, such as a photo.

Using gestures to control Windows

To use your tablet efficiently and accurately, you need to know how to use gestures to control Windows. Using a tablet is a different experience than using a regular computer, but Windows was built with the tablet in mind, so it's intuitive and easy to learn.

If you've never used a tablet PC before, the main difference is that you use your fingers (or stylus) to run applications, select items, and manipulate screen objects. This might seem awkward at first, but it will come to seem quite natural if you practice the techniques shown here as much as you can:

- Swipe left from the right edge of the tablet screen to display the Notifications pane.

- Swipe right from the left edge of the tablet screen to display Task View for switching between running applications and viewing your timeline.

- Swipe (or slide) up, down, left, or right to navigate an app's screens.

- To shut down an app, slide down from the top edge of the screen until the app window turns into a thumbnail, and then slide the thumbnail down to the bottom of the screen.

- To move an item, tap and hold the item and immediately begin moving your finger or the stylus. As you do, the object moves along with your finger or the stylus. When the object is repositioned where you want it, lift your finger or the stylus off the screen to complete the move.

- You can also use the following gestures in File Explorer:

  - Select a single file or folder by tapping it.

  - Select multiple, adjacent files or folders by tapping and holding the screen above and to the left of the first item, and then sliding your finger or stylus down and to the right until you have selected the items you want.

  - Select multiple, nonadjacent files or folders by tapping the check box that appears to the left of each item. If you don't see the check boxes, tap View and then tap to select Item Check Boxes.

Inputting Text with the Touch Keyboard

If you are using a tablet, or a 2-in-1 PC in tablet configuration, you don't have a physical keyboard available. To input text, Windows offers the *touch keyboard*, which is a virtual keyboard that appears on the screen. You input text using this keyboard by tapping the keys. Windows offers several touch keyboard types, and some characters are difficult to find, so you need to know how to use the touch keyboard to get the most out of Windows.

Displaying the touch keyboard

To display the touch keyboard in an app, you have two choices:

- Tap inside whatever box you'll be using to type the text.

- Tap the Touch Keyboard icon that appears in the taskbar's notification area (I pointed out this icon back in Figure 8.1).

Note If you don't see the Touch Keyboard icon in the taskbar, tap and hold the taskbar to display the shortcut menu, and then tap Show Touch Keyboard Button.

Figure 8.3 shows the default touch keyboard layout that appears.

Keyboard Settings

![The default touch keyboard layout]

8.3 The default touch keyboard layout.

Selecting a touch keyboard type

Windows offers several touch keyboard types that you can use. To make the switch, tap the Keyboard Settings icon (pointed out in Figure 8.3) and then tap one of the layouts shown in Figure 8.4 and summarized here:

- **Default.** Tap this icon to use the default layout. You can also tap either Fixed to use a version of the default keyboard that is static across the bottom of the screen or Floating to use a version that you can move by dragging the top part of the keyboard.

- **Compact.** Tap this icon to use the compact layout. This layout is much smaller than the default layout, which makes it easier to see what's on your screen. This is a floating layout.

- **Split.** Tap this icon to use the split layout, where the keys are divided roughly in half, with one half displayed toward the left side of the screen and the other half displayed toward the right. You can work with this layout in either fixed or floating mode.

- **Standard.** Tap this icon to use the standard layout, which is an on-screen representation of a full-size keyboard (see Figure 8.5). It includes familiar keys such as Esc,

Tab, Caps, Shift, Fn, Ctrl, Alt, and Windows. You can work with this layout in either fixed or floating mode.

⦿ **Handwriting panel.** Tap this icon to input text by "writing" on the screen using a stylus (as I discuss later in this chapter). You can work with this layout in either a fixed or floating mode.

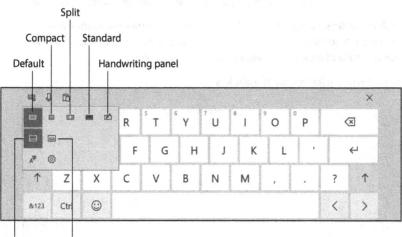

8.4 Tap Keyboard Settings to see the available touch keyboard layouts.

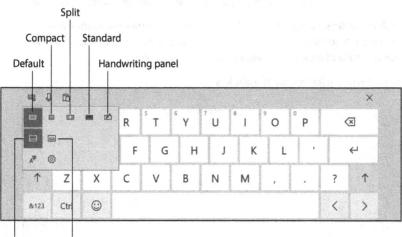

8.5 Tap Standard to see the full-size keyboard shown here.

Using the touch keyboard

With the exception of the handwriting panel (discussed in the next section), inputting text using the touch keyboard is mostly straightforward. That is, once the touch keyboard is on-screen, you enter text by tapping the keys. However, if you're using the default, compact, or split layout, here are a few less-than-obvious techniques you can use:

- To access numbers and other symbols, tap the &123 key to display the keys shown in Figure 8.6 (this is the default layout version).

- To access even more symbols, tap the More key (pointed out in Figure 8.6). You can also tap Back (pointed out in Figure 8.7) to return to the first batch of symbols.

- With many keys, you can tap and hold to see some extra keys, as shown in Figure 8.7. If you see a symbol you want to enter, slide you finger up and over to the symbol and then release your finger from the screen.

- To return to the letters, tap the abc key.

More

8.6 Tap &123 to see numbers and other symbols.

Tap and hold a key to see more symbols

Back   Tap here for even more symbols

8.7 With many keys (such as the © key shown here), you can tap and hold the key to see more symbols.

146

Entering text using the handwriting panel

Most touch or tablet PCs come with a device called a *stylus* (also called a digital pen) that you can use instead of a finger. For example, tapping the screen with a stylus is the same as tapping with a finger or clicking the mouse. However, most people use a stylus to enter text. By pressing lightly on the screen with the stylus, you can insert text by "writing" the characters on the screen using the handwriting panel.

Follow these steps to enter handwritten text using a stylus:

1. **Tap inside the text area where you want to input text.**

2. **On the touch keyboard, tap Keyboard Settings (pointed out earlier in Figure 8.3).** If you don't see the touch keyboard automatically, tap the Touch Keyboard icon in the taskbar (see Figure 8.1).

3. **Tap Handwriting Panel.** I pointed out this icon in Figure 8.4. The touch keyboard switches to the handwriting panel.

4. **Use your stylus to write your text on the screen inside the large text area, as shown in Figure 8.8.** Windows converts what you've written into regular text and inserts the converted characters into the text box (see Figure 8.9) as follows:

   - When you stop or pause writing for at least a couple of seconds, Windows converts what you've written so far.

   - When you leave some space between one handwritten letter and the next (for example, when you're starting a new word), Windows converts the text before the space.

Genius

You can make the handwriting conversion a bit more accurate by telling Windows which hand you use for writing. Open the Settings app, tap Devices, tap Pen & Windows Ink, and then use the Choose Which Hand You Write With list to select either Left Hand or Right Hand.

5. **If the converted text contains an error, you have several choices for fixing the problem:**

   - Tap the Backspace icon (see Figure 8.9) as needed.

   - Overwrite the incorrect characters with the correct text. For example, if I wanted to change *meditation* in Figure 8.9 to *meditating*, I'd overwrite the letters *on* with the letters *ng*.

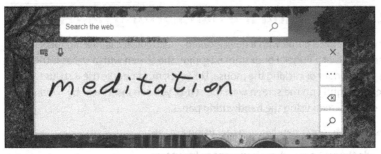

8.8 Use the stylus to write your text within the handwriting panel's large text area.

Windows adds the converted characters to the text box   Backspace

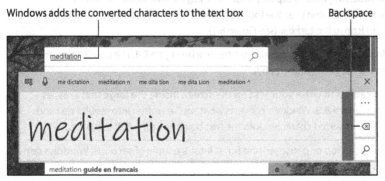

8.9 Windows converts your handwriting into regular text and inserts the characters into the text box.

- To delete one or more characters, use the *strikethrough* gesture: Draw a straight, horizontal line through the characters you want to delete.

- To combine two words into a single word, use the *join* gesture: Draw an arc (like an upside-down U) over the words from the last letter of the first word to the first letter of the second word.

- To create two words out of a single word, use the *split* gesture: Draw a caret (an upside-down V) under the word at the position where you want the split to occur.

Genius

The join gesture also works in the opposite way: That is, you can draw a U-like arc under the words from the last letter of the first word to the first letter of the second word. Similarly, for the split gesture you can also draw a V over the word at the position where you want the split to occur.

Configuring the touch keyboard

The touch keyboard offers a number of features that make it easier to use. For example, the touch keyboard automatically adds a period and space when you double-tap the spacebar, and it automatically capitalizes the first letter of each sentence. However, the touch keyboard also has some features that you might not like—such as the noise it makes each time you tap a key. You can use the Settings app to turn on the touch keyboard features that you like and turn off the features that you don't like:

1. **Tap Start and then tap Settings.** The Settings app appears.

2. **Tap Devices.** The Devices screen appears.

3. **Tap Typing.** The Typing settings appear.

4. **Under Touch Keyboard, tap each switch On or Off, according to your preferences:**

   - **Play key sounds as I type.** This setting is On by default. Tap it to Off to mute the sound the touch keyboard makes as you tap each key.

   - **Capitalize the first letter of each sentence.** This setting is On by default. Tap it to Off to prevent the touch keyboard from automatically capitalizing the first letter of new sentences.

   - **Use all uppercase letters when I double-tap Shift.** This setting is On by default. Tap it to Off to prevent the touch keyboard from locking the Shift key when you double-tap it.

   - **Show the touch keyboard when not in tablet mode and there's no keyboard attached.** This setting is Off by default. Tap it to On to have Windows automatically display the touch keyboard even when your PC isn't in tablet mode (and there's no keyboard connected to your PC).

   Windows applies your new settings to the touch keyboard.

Setting Power and Battery Options

A desktop PC requires a nearby power outlet, but a tablet PC is capable of running off its internal battery for those times when power is nowhere in sight. This enables you to use your tablet almost anywhere, including at a coffee shop, in a taxi, on an airplane, and even at the park. However, to make the most out of this portability, you need to take good care of the tablet battery. This includes tracking battery usage, saving as much energy as possible when you're on battery power, adjusting screen brightness, and more. The rest of this chapter shows you how to perform all these battery-related chores.

Monitoring battery life

You can use the Power icon in the taskbar's notification area to monitor your tablet's remaining battery power. When the battery is at maximum charge, the icon shows as all black, as you can see in Figure 8.10. As the battery charge falls, the amount of black in the icon also falls. For example, Figure 8.11 shows the Power icon when the battery level is at 50 percent.

You can also tap the Power icon to open a window (see Figure 8.12) that shows you the current battery level and the approximate amount of battery life (in hours and minutes) remaining.

Power icon

8.10 The Power icon is completely black when the battery level is at 100 percent.

8.11 The Power icon is half black when the battery level is down to 50 percent.

50% 4 hours 26 minutes remaining

Power mode (on battery): Better performance

Best battery life   Best performance

Battery settings

8.12 Tap the Power icon to see this window.

Genius

If you find your tablet's battery life isn't as good as it once was, a recently installed or updated app might be the culprit. To see if a particular app is using an excessive amount of battery power, open the Settings app, tap System, and then tap Battery. The Battery Usage Per App section gives you an app-by-app battery summary.

Setting the power mode

Working on battery power is a constant tradeoff between battery life and PC performance:

- For best performance, you can leave your hard drive running and your screen on for longer periods, but you'll use up battery resources faster.
- For best battery life, you can have your hard drive and your screen turn off faster, but the overall performance of your PC will suffer (because, for example, you might have to wait a bit while your hard drive or screen come back online).

How you resolve this tradeoff depends on how you work and whether a power outlet is nearby. To tell Windows your preference, you set the *power mode*, which configures Windows for better battery life or better performance.

To set the power mode, tap the Power icon to display the window shown earlier in Figure 8.12, then drag the Power Mode slider to the setting you prefer.

Adjusting screen brightness

You can extend the battery life of your tablet by turning down the screen brightness. Your tablet screen uses a lot of power, so turning down the brightness also reduces battery drain.

On the other hand, if you have trouble seeing the data on your tablet screen, you can often fix the problem by increasing the screen brightness. This is not a problem when your tablet is running on power. However, you shouldn't use full screen brightness for very long when your tablet is running on its battery because a bright screen uses a lot of power.

To adjust the screen brightness, follow these steps:

1. **Tap Action Center.** I pointed out this taskbar icon earlier in Figure 8.1. Windows opens the Action Center.

2. **If you don't see all the Action Center tiles (that is, if you see only a row of four tiles at the bottom of the Action Center), tap Expand.** Action Center displays all of its actions (as shown earlier in Figure 8.2).

3. **Tap and drag the brightness slider to set the brightness as you prefer it.** Windows puts the new brightness setting into effect.

Switching to Battery Saver mode

If your tablet's battery is running low and there's no power outlet around, you need to conserve battery power. For example, you could switch Power Mode to Best Battery Life (that is, drag the Power Mode slider shown in Figure 8.12 all the way to the left) and you could reduce the tablet's screen brightness (as I describe in the previous section).

Another useful technique is to switch your tablet to Battery Saver mode, which reduces the number of notifications you see, turns off most background tasks, and performs a few other tweaks to extend overall battery life.

By default, Windows automatically switches into Battery Saver mode when your battery life drops to 20 percent. However, you can use either of the following techniques to switch to Battery Saver mode at any time:

- Tap Action Center and then tap to activate the Battery Saver action.

- Open the Settings app, tap System, tap Battery, and then tap the Battery Saver switch to On. While you're here, you can also use the Turn Battery Saver On Automatically At list to select a percentage of battery life when you want Windows to switch automatically to Battery Saver mode.

Note

Another way to get to the Battery settings is to tap the taskbar's Power icon and then tap the Battery Settings link.

Creating a custom power plan to improve battery life

When you use a tablet on battery power, you always have to choose between increased battery life and tablet performance. For example, to increase battery life, Windows shuts down components, such as the display, or switches to sleep mode after a short time. If you find that Windows turns off the screen too quickly or too slowly, or switches to sleep mode too soon or too late, follow these steps to adjust these times to suit your needs:

1. **Tap Start and then tap Settings.**

2. **Tap System.**

3. **Tap Power & Sleep.** The Power & Sleep settings appear, as shown in Figure 8.13.

4. **In the Screen section, use the On Battery Power, Turn Off After list to choose the idle interval after which Windows turns off the tablet display while running on battery power.**

5. **In the Sleep section, use the On Battery Power, PC Goes to Sleep After list to choose the idle interval after which Windows puts the tablet to sleep while running on battery power.**

Power & sleep

Screen

On battery power, turn off after

| 10 minutes ∨ |

When plugged in, turn off after

| 30 minutes ∨ |

Sleep

On battery power, PC goes to sleep after

| 30 minutes ∨ |

When plugged in, PC goes to sleep after

| 30 minutes ∨ |

Home

Find a setting

System

Display

Sound

Notifications & actions

Focus assist

Power & sleep

Battery

Storage

Tablet

8.13 Use the Power & Sleep setting to create a custom power plan for your tablet PC.

6. **While you're on the Power & Sleep page, note that you can also configure intervals for the screen and sleep mode that Windows uses when your tablet PC is plugged in:**

- In the Screen section, use the When Plugged In, Turn Off After list to choose the idle interval after which Windows turns off the tablet display while your device is plugged in.

- In the Sleep section, use the When Plugged In, PC Goes to Sleep After list to choose the idle interval after which Windows puts the tablet to sleep while your tablet is plugged in.

Checking out more ways to save energy

Even with the energy settings optimized for longer battery life, you can still do a few other things to keep your tablet running longer. Generally, this means turning off or closing anything you don't need while running on battery power. Here are some suggestions:

- **Quit any unneeded applications.** Running programs may still use up some processor cycles, even when you're not actively using them. For example, your email program may check for new messages every so often. To avoid these power drains, you should shut down any application unnecessary for your work.

- **Minimize your tasks.** Avoid secondary chores, such as checking for software updates and organizing your music library. If your only goal is to finish your presentation, stick to that until it's done (given that you don't know how much time you'll have).

- **Sleep your tablet by hand, if necessary.** If you get interrupted—for example, the in-flight meal arrives—don't wait for Windows to put itself to sleep, because those few minutes will use up precious battery time. Instead, put your tablet to sleep manually right away by either closing the lid or by tapping Power and then Sleep.

- **Disconnect any devices you don't need.** Even an unused device can drain battery power, so if you have anything connected to a tablet port, disconnect it.

- **Turn off Wi-Fi if you don't need it.** When Wi-Fi is on, it regularly checks for available wireless networks, which drains the battery. If you don't need to connect to a wireless network, turn off Wi-Fi to conserve energy. Open the Settings app, tap Network & Internet, tap Wi-Fi, and then tap the Wi-Fi switch to Off.

- **Turn off Bluetooth if you don't need it.** When Bluetooth is running, it constantly checks for nearby Bluetooth devices and this drains the battery. If you aren't using any Bluetooth devices, turn off Bluetooth to save energy. Open the Settings app, tap Devices, and then tap the Bluetooth switch to Off.

- **Use simple applications to accomplish simple tasks.** For example, if you're just typing a to-do list, you don't need to fire up Microsoft Word—use Notepad instead.

How Do I Work with Documents?

To be productive with Windows, you need to know how to work with the files that you create on your PC. That is, you need to learn how to deal with documents. In this chapter, you begin by learning the most common document chores, including creating, saving, and opening documents. You then learn how to edit document text, find and replace text, and more. From there you learn the basics of working with OneNote notebooks. Finally, you learn how to work with any file on your PC, including copying, moving, renaming, and deleting files.

Editing Documents. **158**

Taking Notes with OneNote. **168**

Working with Files **175**

Editing Documents

A *document* is a file that you or someone else created using an app. For example, a word processing document is one that was created using a word processing app such as WordPad; similarly, a notebook is a document that was created using OneNote. You likely create and use documents constantly when working with your PC, so knowing how to create, save, and edit these documents will make you more productive.

Creating a new document

When you're ready to create something using Windows, in most cases you begin by launching an app and then using that app to create a new document to hold your work. Many Windows apps (such as WordPad and Paint 3D) create a new document for you automatically when you begin the program. However, you can also use these apps to create another new document after you've started the app.

In most apps, you can use either of the following techniques to create a new document:

- Click File and then click New.
- Press Ctrl+N.

Note

You can also create a new file directly from File Explorer. You learn how later in this chapter.

Saving a document

As you work on a document, Windows stores the changes in your computer's memory. However, Windows erases your PC's memory whenever you shut down or restart the computer. How do you preserve your changes? You do so by saving the document, which preserves your changes on your computer's hard drive.

For an existing document, saving your work means just running the app's Save command. However, for a new document that hasn't yet been saved, you need to jump through a few more hoops, as the following steps show:

1. **In the app you're using, click File and then click Save.** If you saved the document previously, your changes are now preserved, so you don't need to follow the rest of the steps in this section. If this is a new document that you've never saved before, the Save As dialog box appears, as shown in Figure 9.1.

9.1 In most apps, you use the Save As dialog box to save a new document to your PC's hard drive.

Note In most apps, you can also press Ctrl+S or click the Save button on the app's toolbar.

2. **Open the Documents folder.** In most apps, the Documents folder is selected automatically when you save a document.

3. **(Optional) Open the subfolder in which you want to store the file.**

Genius If needed, you can create a subfolder within Documents. In the Save As dialog box, click New Folder, type the name of the folder, press Enter, double-click the new folder to open it, and then follow Steps 4 and 5.

4. **Use the File Name text box to type the name you want to use for the document.** The name you type can be up to 255 characters long, but it can't include the following characters: < > , ? : " \ *.

5. **Click Save.** The app saves your document in the folder you specified.

Opening a document

When you save a document, you save its contents to your PC's hard drive, and those contents are stored in a separate file. When you open the document using the same app that you used to save it, Windows loads the file's contents into memory and displays the document in the app. You can then view or edit the document as needed.

Here are the steps to follow in most apps to open a document:

1. **Start the app you want to work with.**

2. **Click File.** If you see the document you want in a list of the most recently used documents on the File menu, you can click the name to open it. You can then skip the rest of the steps in this section.

3. **Click Open.** The Open dialog box appears.

Note

In most apps, you can also press Ctrl+O or click the Open button on the app's toolbar.

4. **(Optional) Click Documents.** This step is optional because in most apps, the Documents folder is selected automatically when you open a document. Windows displays the contents of the Documents folder.

5. **(Optional) If the document you want to open resides in a subfolder, open that subfolder.**

6. **Select the document you want to open.**

7. **Click Open.** The document appears in the app window.

Note

You don't always need to open the app first. Instead, use File Explorer to open the folder that contains the document and then double-click the document. Windows automatically launches the app (assuming it's not running already) and opens the document.

Genius

If you're not sure where a document resides on your hard drive, Windows offers a document search feature, which is also handy if your Documents folder contains many files. Use the taskbar's Search box to type some or all of the document's filename and then click the Documents tab.

Changing the text font

You can add visual appeal to a document by changing the font formatting. The font formatting includes attributes such as the typeface, style, size, and special effects:

- A *typeface*—also called a *font*—is a distinctive character design that you can apply to the selected text in a document.

- The *type style* refers to formatting applied to text, such as **bold** or *italics*.

- The *type size* refers to the height of each character, which is measured in *points*; 72 points equal one inch.

- *Special effects* are styles that change the appearance of the text, such as <u>underline</u> and ~~strikethrough~~.

How you apply font formatting varies from one app to another, but the following steps work in most apps:

1. **Select the text you want to format.**

2. **Display the font options.** In WordPad, shown in Figure 9.2, you display the font options by clicking the Home tab. In many other apps, you display the font options by clicking Format in the menu bar and then clicking the Font command.

Font Family   Font Size

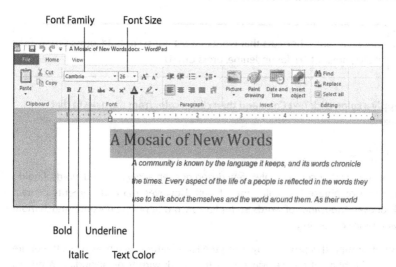

Bold   Underline

Italic   Text Color

9.2 In WordPad, the font formatting commands appear on the Home tab.

3. **Use the Font list to choose the typeface you want.**

4. **Use the Size list to choose the type size you want.**

5. **For bold text, click the Bold button.**

6. **For italics, click the Italic button.**

161

Using Fonts Responsibly

Here are some guidelines to follow when working with fonts in your documents:

- Use at most one or two typefaces to avoid the "ransom note" look.
- Avoid overly decorative typefaces because they're often difficult to read.
- Use bold only for document titles, subtitles, and headings.
- Use italics only to emphasize words and phrases, or for the titles of books and magazines.
- Use larger type sizes only for document titles, subtitles, and, possibly, headings.
- In general, dark text on a light background is the easiest to read (the darker the text and the lighter the background, the better).

7. For underlining, click the Underline button.

Genius

Here are some shortcuts that work in most apps: For bold, press Ctrl+B; for italics, press Ctrl+I; for underline, press Ctrl+U.

8. To apply a color, click Text Color and then click a color from the palette that appears.

Finding text

In short documents that contain only a few dozen or even a few hundred words, finding a specific word or phrase is usually not difficult. However, many documents contain hundreds or even thousands of words, so finding a word or phrase becomes much more difficult and time consuming.

You can work around this problem by using the Find feature, which searches the entire document in the blink of an eye. Most apps that work with text—including Windows WordPad and Notepad apps—have the Find feature.

Follow these steps to use Find to locate text in a document:

1. Click Find. In WordPad, shown in Figure 9.3, you display the Editing options by clicking the Home tab. The Find dialog box appears.

Note

In many apps, you run the Find command by clicking Edit in the menu bar and then clicking the Find command, or by pressing Ctrl+F.

2. **Use the Find What text box to type the text you want to find.**

3. **Click Find Next.** The app selects the next instance of the search text, as shown in Figure 9.3. If the search text doesn't exist in the document, the app displays a dialog box to let you know.

The Find command

9.3 Use the Find feature to locate a word in a document.

4. **If the selected instance is not the one you want, click Find Next until the app finds the correct instance.**

5. **When you're done, click Close (X) to close the Find dialog box.** The app leaves the found text selected.

Genius

You might find that a search for a word such as *the* also matches larger words such as *theme* and *bother*. To avoid this, click the Match Whole Word Only check box. This tells the app to match the search text only if it's a word on its own.

Genius

If you're trying to search for a name such as *Bill*, you can avoid matching the non-name *bill* by clicking the Match Case check box. This tells the app to match the search text only if it has the same mix of uppercase and lowercase letters that you specify in the Find What text box.

Replacing text

Do you need to replace a word or part of a word with some other text? Making one or two replacements isn't onerous, but if you have several instances to replace, you can save time and do a more accurate job if you let the app's Replace feature replace the word for you. Most apps that work with text—including the WordPad and Notepad apps—include the Replace feature.

Follow these steps to use Replace to replace text in a document:

1. **Click Replace.** In WordPad, shown in Figure 9.4, you display the Editing options by clicking the Home tab. The Replace dialog box appears.

Note

In many apps, you run the Replace command by clicking Edit in the menu bar and then clicking the Replace command, or by pressing Ctrl+H.

The Replace command

The Jargon of Junk Food

Most of us love food—many of us love food a little *too*
dangerous rates of morbid obesity in the United States
an epidemic known as *globesity*. Those extra pounds
from the over-consumption of pop, snack foods, and
The massive popularity of these so-called *junk foods* (
added to the language menu in 1973) is a testament t
industry's talent for creating feel-good food.

Our diets may be richer for it, but so too is the English language, which
now boasts many tasty new words and phrases cooked up by food
industry scientists and technologists.

9.4 Use the Replace feature to replace one word with another.

Replacing All Instances

If you're certain you want to replace every instance of the search text with the replacement text, click Replace All. This tells the app to replace every instance of the search text with the replacement text. However, you should exercise some caution with this feature because it may make some replacements that you didn't intend. Click Find Next a few times to make sure the matches are correct. Also, consider clicking the Match Whole Word Only and Match Case check boxes, as described in the previous section, to ensure the text more exactly matches what's replaced.

2. **Use the Find What text box to type the text you want to find.**

3. **Use the Replace With text box to type the text you want to use as the replacement.**

4. **Click Find Next.** The app selects the next instance of the search text, as shown in Figure 9.4. If the search text doesn't exist in the document, the app displays a dialog box to let you know.

5. **If the selected instance is not the one you want, click Find Next until the app finds the correct instance.**

6. **Click Replace.** The app replaces the selected text with the replacement text and then selects the next instance of the search text.

7. **Repeat Steps 5 and 6 until you have replaced all the instances you want to replace.**

8. **When you're done, click Close (X) to close the Replace dialog box.**

Inserting special symbols

The keyboard is home to a large number of letters, numbers, and symbols. However, the keyboard is missing some useful characters. For example, it's missing the foreign characters in words such as café and Köln. Similarly, your writing might require mathematical symbols such as ÷ and ½, financial symbols such as € and ¥, or commercial symbols such as ™ and ©. You can make your documents more readable and more useful by inserting these and any of the many other symbols that are available in Windows via the Character Map app. Here are the steps to follow:

1. **Click Start, click Windows Accessories, and then click Character Map.**
   Alternatively, use the taskbar's Search box to type **char** and then click Character Map in the search results. Either way, the Character Map window appears.

2. Click the symbol you want to insert.

3. Click Select. Character Map adds the symbol to the Characters to Copy text box, as shown in Figure 9.5.

Genius

In Figure 9.5, notice that Character Map displays a "keystroke" in the status bar (Alt+0169, in this case). This tells you that you can insert the symbol directly into your document by pressing the keystroke shown. For example, you can insert the copyright symbol (©) by pressing Alt+0169. When you type the numbers, be sure to use your keyboard's numeric keypad.

9.5 Use Character Map to insert special symbols into a document.

4. Repeat Steps 2 and 3 for any other characters you want to insert.

5. Click Copy. Character Map places the character(s) in the Clipboard.

6. Click Close (X) to shut down Character Map.

7. Switch to your document and position the cursor where you want to insert the symbol.

8. Click the app's Paste command. The app inserts the character(s) into the document.

Genius

Dozens of extra symbols are available in the Character Map app's Webdings and Wingdings typefaces. To see these symbols, use the Font list to choose Webdings or Wingdings.

Saving a copy of a document

When you need to create a document that's nearly identical to an existing document, instead of creating the new document from scratch, you can save time by saving a copy of the existing document and then modifying the copy as needed. For example, you might have a résumé cover letter that you want to modify for a different job application. Similarly, this year's conference agenda is likely to be similar to last year's. Instead of creating these new documents from scratch, it's much faster to use the app's Save As command to save a copy of the original document and then edit the copy as needed. Here are the steps to follow to save a copy of a document:

1. **Start the app you want to work with and open the original document.**

2. **Click File and then click Save As.** The Save As dialog box appears.

3. **Open the Documents folder.** In most apps, the Documents folder is selected automatically when you run the Save As command.

4. **(Optional) Open the subfolder in which you want to store the new file.**

Genius

If needed, you can create a subfolder within Documents. In the Save As dialog box, click New Folder, type the name of the folder, press Enter, double-click the new folder to open it, and then follow Steps 5 and 6.

5. **Use the File Name text box to type the name you want to use for the new document.** The name you type can be up to 255 characters long, but it can't include the following characters: < > , ? : " \ *.

6. **Click Save.** The app closes the original document and opens the copy you just created.

Genius

Save As can operate as a rudimentary backup tool. Create a copy with the same name as the original but store the copy in a different location. Good places to choose are your OneDrive, a USB flash drive, or a memory card. Remember, too, that after you complete the Save As steps, the backup copy will be open in the app. Be sure to close the copy and then reopen the original.

Taking Notes with OneNote

You can use the OneNote app to record and save miscellaneous bits of information, including text, lists, drawings, images, web pages, and tables of data. All of this is stored in a special document called a *notebook*. Within each notebook you can organize your data within *sections*, where each section is devoted to a particular subject. Each section is then divided into one or more *pages*, and you use these pages to enter your data.

Note

Your Windows user account must be connected to a Microsoft account to use OneNote.

Creating a OneNote notebook

OneNote creates a notebook for you automatically when you first launch the app. If you want to create another notebook, follow these steps:

1. **Click Start and then click OneNote.**

2. **Click Get Started.** The OneNote app appears.

3. **Click** *Name's* **Notebook, where** *Name* **is your first name.**

4. **Click Add Notebook.** The New Notebook dialog box appears.

5. **Click the right side of the screen.**

6. **Type a name for the notebook.**

7. **Click Create Notebook.** OneNote creates a new notebook and populates it with a single section (named Quick Notes) and an untitled page, as shown in Figure 9.6.

Genius

If you want to delete a notebook, you must use the online version of OneNote. Sign in to onedrive.live.com. Click Documents, position the mouse pointer over the OneNote notebook, and then click the file's check box. Click Delete in the toolbar.

Adding pages and sections to a notebook

You can keep your notes organized and easy to find by taking advantage of OneNote's pages and sections. You can add as many sections and pages as you need to keep your notes organized.

Section tabs   Page list   Type the page title here

9.6 A new notebook displayed in the OneNote app.

Adding a section to a notebook

Each OneNote notebook consists of one or more sections, which you use to break down the notebook's overall topic or theme into smaller, more manageable subjects. Follow these steps to add a section to the notebook:

1. **Click Add Section.** OneNote adds a section to the notebook. OneNote populates the new section with a blank, untitled page.

2. **Type the section name and press Enter.** OneNote sets the section title.

Note

If you need to rename a section, right-click the section tab, click Rename Section, type the new name, and then press Enter.

Note

To change a section's color scheme, right-click the section tab, click Section Color, and then click the color you want to use.

Adding a page to a notebook

You can further break down each section into one or more pages, which are the OneNote items within which you add text, images, lists, and other data. Follow these steps to insert a new page into a section:

1. **Click the section in which you want to add the page.**

2. **Click Add page.** OneNote adds a page to the section.

3. **Type a title for the page (see Figure 9.6) and press Enter.** OneNote sets the page title.

Note

To rename a page, right-click the page in the Pages list, click Rename Page, type the new name, and then press Enter.

Note

To delete a page, right-click the page in the Pages list and then click Delete Page.

Adding and working with text notes

Once you have your sections and pages, your next step is to fill your pages with content. OneNote makes it easy to insert everything from simple text notes to pictures to entire files. All OneNote content appears inside a *container*, which is essentially a box that surrounds the content. After you have some content inside a container, you can move the container around on the page, edit or format the container content, and more.

Adding a text note

Most page content consists of text notes, and OneNote makes it very simple to add text to a page, as the following steps show:

1. **Click the section you want to use.**

2. **Click the page you want to use.**

3. **Click inside the page at the position where you want the text to appear.** OneNote adds an insertion point cursor.

4. **Type your text.** OneNote adds a container around your text, as shown in Figure 9.7.

Font Formatting

9.7 A text note and its container.

5. **When your text note is complete, click outside the container.** OneNote adds the text note to the page.

> **Note**
> To format note text, select the text you want to work with and then click the Home tab to display the text note formatting options. You can click Bold, Italic, or Underline to apply those font styles to the text. You can also use the Font Formatting list (pointed out in Figure 9.7) to see other formatting options such as the font, size, and strikethrough effect.

Sizing a text note container

Follow these steps to change the size of a text note container:

1. **Position the mouse pointer over the right edge of the container.** The pointer changes to a horizontal, two-headed arrow.

2. **Click and drag the mouse pointer to the right for a larger container, or to the left for a smaller container.**

3. **When the container is the size you want, release the mouse.** OneNote resizes the container and adjusts the text to fit the new size.

Moving a text note container

Follow these steps to move a text note container:

1. **Position the mouse pointer over the top edge of the container.** The pointer changes to a four-headed arrow.

2. **Click and drag the mouse pointer to move the container.**

3. **When the container is in the position you want, release the mouse.** OneNote moves the container to the new position.

Adding an image to a notebook page

Although you'll likely populate your OneNote notebooks mostly with text notes, you can also insert other types of content, including images. You can either insert an image file from your PC's hard drive or, if your computer has a camera attached, take a photo and insert it directly into the page. As with text notes, OneNote adds an image to the page within a container that you can move and size as needed. Follow these steps to add an image to a page:

1. **Click the section you want to use.**

2. **Click the page you want to use.**

3. **Click inside the page at the position where you want the image to appear.**

4. **Click the Insert tab.**

5. **Click Pictures and then click From File.** The Open dialog box appears. If you want to add a photo using your PC's camera, you can click From Camera, instead. If the image file is on the web, click From Online.

6. **Click the image file you want to insert.**

7. **Click Open.** OneNote inserts the image into the page and adds a container around your image.

Genius
To add a title for the image, click the image, press Enter, and then type the title above the image. To add a caption, click inside the space just below the image (but still in the image container) and then type your caption.

Genius
To insert other types of files, such as PDF files, text files, and Microsoft Office documents, follow Steps 1 to 4, click File, choose the file, and then click Open.

Working with notebook lists

Many OneNote notes consist of lists of items: shopping lists, to-do lists, books read, movies watched, and so on.

Creating a bulleted list

If you have a list that doesn't require a particular sequence, you can add the items to a page as a bulleted list. Here are the steps to follow:

1. **Click the section you want to use.**

2. **Click the page you want to use.**

3. **Click inside the page at the position where you want the list to appear.**

4. **Click the Home tab.**

5. **Click Bullets.** I point out this icon in Figure 9.8. OneNote adds the list to a container.

6. **Click inside the container and type your list items, pressing Enter after each item.** Figure 9.8 shows an example of a bulleted list.

7. **When you're done, click outside the container.** OneNote adds the bulleted list to the page.

9.8 A bulleted list in a notebook page.

Creating a numbered list

If you have a list that does require a sequence, then you can add the items to the page as a numbered list. Here are the steps to follow:

1. **Click the section you want to use.**

2. **Click the page you want to use.**

3. **Click inside the page at the position where you want the list to appear.**

4. **Click the Home tab.**

5. **Click Numbering.** I point out this icon in Figure 9.8. OneNote adds the list to a container.

6. **Click inside the container and type your list items, pressing Enter after each item.**

7. **When you're done, click outside the container.** OneNote adds the numbered list to the page.

Creating a to-do list

One of the most common OneNote list types is the to-do list, which is a collection of tasks, each with a leading check box. When you complete a task, you activate its check box. Follow these steps to create a to-do list:

1. **Click the section you want to use.**

2. **Click the page you want to use.**

3. **Click inside the page at the position where you want the list to appear.**

4. **Add each item that you want to include in your to-do list, pressing Enter after each item so that the items all appear on a separate line within the container.**

5. **Select all the items in the list.**

6. **On the Home tab, click To Do.** I point out this icon in Figure 9.9. OneNote adds a check box to the left of each item.

9.9 A to-do list in a notebook page.

Genius

Besides To Do, OneNote offers four other tag types: Important, Question, Remember for Later, and Definition. To apply one of these tags, select the text, click Home, and then click the arrow to the right of To Do to click the tag. To create your own tag, click Create New Tag, type a name for the tag, click a tag icon, and then click Create.

Working with Files

This section shows you how to work with the files on your computer. These easy and efficient methods show you how to view, select, copy, move, rename, and delete files, as well as how to restore accidentally deleted files, how to extract files from a compressed folder, and more.

Selecting a file

Before you can use File Explorer to do any work with one or more files, you first have to select the files so that Windows knows which ones you want to work with. For example, before you can move files to a new location, you must first select the files you want to move. You can select just a single file, two or more files, a group of files, or all the files in a folder.

Note

Although you learn specifically about selecting files in this section, the technique for selecting folders is exactly the same.

Here are the techniques you can use to select one or more files in File Explorer:

- **Select a single file.** Open the folder containing the file and then click the file.

- **Select multiple files.** Open the folder containing the files, click the first file you want to select, press and hold Ctrl, and then click each of the other files you want to select.

- **Select a group of files.** Open the folder containing the files, position the mouse pointer slightly above and slightly to the left of the first file in the group, then click and drag the mouse pointer down and to the right until all the files in the group are selected.

- **Select all files.** Open the folder containing the files, click the Home tab, and then click Select All.

A quick way to select all the files in a folder is to press Ctrl+A.

Changing the file view

You can configure how Windows displays the files in a folder by changing the file view. This enables you to see larger or smaller icons or the details of each file. You can choose a view such as Small Icons to see more files in the folder window. A view such as Large Icons or Extra Large Icons enables you to view images as thumbnail versions of each picture. If you want to see more information about the files, choose either the Tiles view or Details view.

Follow these steps to change the view in File Explorer:

1. **Open the folder containing the files you want to view.**

2. **Click the View tab.**

3. **In the Layout section (see Figure 9.10), click the view you want.** File Explorer changes the file view.

			File Explorer
File	Home	Share	View

Navigation pane ▼	Preview pane	Extra large icons	Large icons	Medium icons
	Details pane	Small icons	List	Details
		Tiles	Content	
Panes		Layout		

9.10 In File Explorer's View tab, choose a file view from the Layout section.

Previewing a file

Windows enables you to view the contents of some files without opening them. This makes it easier to select the file you want to work with because it means you do not have to run an application to see the file's contents. Previewing the file is faster and uses fewer system resources. Windows previews only certain types of files, such as text documents, rich text documents, web pages, images, and videos.

Follow these steps to preview a file in File Explorer:

1. **Open the folder containing the file you want to preview.**

2. **Click the View tab.**

3. **Choose Preview Pane.** The Preview pane appears.

Genius

You can also press Alt+P to open the Preview pane.

4. **Click a file.** The file's contents appear in the Preview pane, as shown in Figure 9.11. You can click and drag the left edge of the Preview pane to change its size. When you're finished with the Preview pane, you can deselect Preview Pane on the View tab (or press Alt+P) to close it.

Drag the left edge to resize the Preview pane

9.11 File Explorer's Preview pane in action.

Copying a file

You can use Windows to make an exact copy of a file. This is useful if you want to back up an important file by making an extra copy on a flash drive or memory card. Similarly, you might require a copy of a file if you want to send the copy on a flash drive to another person.

Note

This section shows you how to copy a single file, but the steps also work when you select multiple files. You can also use these steps to copy a folder.

Follow these steps to copy a file in File Explorer:

1. **Open the folder containing the file you want to copy.**

2. **Select the file.**

3. **Click the Home tab.**

4. **Click Copy.** Windows places a copy of the file in a special memory location called the Clipboard.

Genius

You can also press Ctrl+C to copy the file.

5. **Open the location you want to use to store the copy.**

6. **Click the Home tab.**

7. **Click Paste.** Windows inserts a copy of the file in the location.

Genius

You can also press Ctrl+P to paste the file.

Moving a file

When you save a file for the first time, you specify a folder on your PC's hard drive. This original location is not permanent; you can move the file to another location on the hard drive.

This section shows you how to move a single file, but the steps also work if you select multiple files or move a folder.

Follow these steps to move a file in File Explorer:

1. **Open the folder containing the file you want to move.**

2. **Select the file or files.**

3. **Click the Home tab.**

4. **Click Cut.** Windows places the file in the Clipboard.

Genius

You can also press Ctrl+X to cut the file.

5. **Open the location where you want to move the file.**

6. **Click the Home tab.**

7. **Click Paste.** Windows moves the file to the new location.

Genius

You can also press Ctrl+V to paste the file.

Renaming a document

You can change the name of a document, which is useful if the current name of the file doesn't accurately describe or reflect its contents. By giving your document a descriptive or accurate name, you make it easier both to find the file later and to know what the file contains.

Caution

Make sure you rename only those documents that you've created or that someone else has given to you. Do *not* rename any of the Windows system files or any files associated with your apps, or your computer may behave erratically, or even crash.

Here are the steps to follow to rename a document:

1. **In File Explorer, open the folder that contains the file you want to rename.**

2. **Click the file.** In addition to renaming files, you can also rename any folders that you've created.

3. **Click the Home tab and then click Rename.** A text box appears around the filename.

Genius

You can also press F2 to run the Rename command.

4. **Type the new name you want to use for the file.** The name you type can be up to 255 characters long, but it can't include the following characters: < > , ? : " \ *. If you decide that you do not want to rename the file after all, press Esc to cancel the operation.

5. **Press Enter or click an empty section of the folder.** The new name appears under the file's icon.

Creating a new file

You can quickly create a new file directly within a file folder. This method is faster, and often more convenient, than running an app's New command (as I describe earlier). In Windows, you can create several different file types, such as a Bitmap Image (a drawing), Rich Text Document (a WordPad file), Text Document (a Notepad file), and Compressed (Zipped) Folder (which combines multiple files in a single file, as described later in this chapter). You can also create a new folder.

Here are the steps to follow to create a new file:

1. **In File Explorer, open the folder in which you want to create the file.**

2. **Click the Home tab and then, in the New section, click New Item.** File Explorer displays a menu of file types. The New Item menu on your system may contain extra items because some apps install their own file types. For example, if you have Microsoft Office installed, you see items for creating a Word document, an Excel workbook, and more, as shown in Figure 9.12.

	☑	▢	▾	Budget

File | Home | Share | View

Pin to Quick access | Copy | Paste | ✂ Cut | 📋 Copy path | 📄 Paste shortcut | Move to ▾ | Copy to ▾ | 🗑 | ✖ | 🔧 | 🗋 New item ▾

Clipboard | | | | Orga

📁 Folder
🔗 Shortcut
🗃 Microsoft Access Database
🖼 Bitmap image
📄 Microsoft Word Document
🗃 Microsoft Access Database
📊 Microsoft PowerPoint Presentation
📘 Microsoft Publisher Document
📄 Rich Text Format
📄 Text Document
📊 Microsoft Excel Worksheet
🗜 Compressed (zipped) Folder

← → ⌄ ↑ 🖥 › This PC › Documents › Budget

☐ Name ˄

⭐ Quick access
🖥 Desktop 📌
⬇ Downloads 📌
📄 Documents 📌
🖼 Pictures 📌

☁ OneDrive

🖥 This PC

🖧 Network

9.12 File Explorer's New Item menu often contains extra items, such as the Microsoft Office document types shown here.

3. **Click the type of file you want to create.** An icon for the new file appears in the folder.

Genius

If you click Folder in the New Item list, Windows creates a new subfolder. However, note that the Home tab's New section also includes a New Folder icon, which you can click as a faster method for creating a new subfolder.

4. **Type the name you want to use for the new file.** The name you type can be up to 255 characters long, but it can't include the following characters: < > , ? : " \ *.

5. **Press Enter or click an empty section of the folder.** You can now use your new document.

Deleting a document

When you have a document that you no longer need, instead of leaving the file on your hard drive, you can delete it. This not only reduces the clutter on your hard drive, it also creates more space to store new documents.

Caution

Make sure that you delete only those documents that you've created or that someone else has given to you. Do *not* delete any of the Windows system files or any files associated with your apps, or your computer may behave erratically or crash.

Here are the steps to follow to delete a document:

1. **In File Explorer, open the folder that contains the file you want to delete.**

2. **Click the file you want to delete.** If you need to remove more than one file, select all the files you want to delete; see earlier in this chapter to learn how to select multiple files.

3. **Click the Home tab and then click the top half of the Delete button (the red X).** Windows removes the file from the folder and stores it in the Recycle Bin. (If you're sure you never want to recover the file, you can click the lower half of the Delete button and then click Permanently Delete from the menu that appears.)

Genius

You can also press the Delete key to run the Delete command. Another way to delete a document is to click and drag it to the Desktop's Recycle Bin icon.

Restoring a Deleted File

If you delete a file in error, Windows enables you to restore the file by placing it back in the folder from which you deleted it. You can restore a deleted file because Windows stores each deleted file in a special folder called the Recycle Bin, where the file stays for a few days or a few weeks, depending on how often you empty the bin or how full the folder becomes. Follow these steps to restore a file from the Recycle Bin:

1. **On the Desktop, double-click the Recycle Bin icon.** The Recycle Bin folder appears. If you have a tablet or touch PC, open File Explorer, click the first right-pointing arrow in the address bar, and then click Recycle Bin.

2. **Click the file you want to restore.**

3. **Click the Recycle Bin Tools tab.**

4. **Click Restore the Selected Items.** Windows moves the files from the Recycle Bin to its original folder.

Extracting files from a compressed folder

If someone sends you a file via email, or if you download a file from the Internet, the file often arrives in a *compressed* form, which means the file actually contains one or more files that have been reduced in size to save space. To use the files on your computer, you need to extract them from the compressed file.

Because a compressed file can contain one or more files, it acts like a kind of folder. Therefore, Windows calls such files *compressed folders*, *zipped folders*, or *Zip archives*. You can view these files or extract them from the folder.

Caution

Be careful with any ZIP files you receive via email or download from the Internet because such files can harbor viruses and other malware. If you receive the file from a stranger or a website you don't trust, delete it immediately. If you know the person or trust the site where the file comes from, view the ZIP contents before you extract them to make sure the archive doesn't contain anything suspicious.

Viewing compressed folder files

Follow these steps to view the files contained in a compressed folder:

1. **In File Explorer, open the folder containing the compressed folder.** The compressed folder appears as a folder icon with a zipper, as shown in Figure 9.13.

2. **Double-click the compressed folder.** File Explorer displays the contents of the compressed folder, as shown in Figure 9.14.

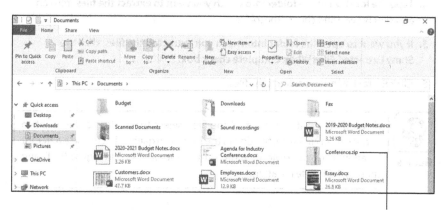

Compressed folder

9.13 Compressed folders appear in File Explorer as a folder icon with a zipper.

183

![Conference.zip window showing compressed folder contents in File Explorer with Extract tab highlighted]

Agenda for Industry Conference.docx — Microsoft Word Document

Conference Schedule.doc — DOC File — 150 KB

Product Ideas.doc — DOC File — 30.0 KB

Survey Results.DOC — DOC File — 18.5 KB

Committee Questions.doc — DOC File — 19.0 KB

Map to Convention Center.doc — DOC File — 32.0 KB

Questions.doc — DOC File — 19.0 KB

Conference Attendees.doc — DOC File — 4.50 KB

Party Invitation.docx — Microsoft Word Document — 434 KB

Speech Notes.DOC — DOC File — 6.50 KB

More

9.14 Double-click a compressed folder to view the files it contains.

Extracting files from a compressed folder

When you open a compressed folder, File Explorer only displays the contents of the compressed folder; it hasn't extracted the files. To extract the files, follow these steps:

1. **In File Explorer, follow the steps in the previous section to open the compressed folder.**

2. **Click the Compressed Folder Tools tab.** This tab should already be selected.

3. **Click Extract all.** The Select a Destination and Extract Files dialog box of the Extract Wizard appears.

4. **Type the location of the folder into which you want to extract the files.** You can also click Browse and choose the folder.

5. **If you want to open the folder into which you extracted the files, click the Show Extracted Files When Complete check box.**

6. **Click Extract.** Windows extracts the files.

Genius

If you don't want to extract all the files, select those files you do want to extract, then click a destination in the Extract To gallery. To choose a different location, click the gallery's More button (pointed out in Figure 9.14) and then click Choose Location.

Creating a compressed folder

If you want to create your own compressed folder, follow these steps:

1. **In File Explorer, select the files and folders you want to store in the compressed folder.**

2. **Right-click any selected item.**

3. **Click Send To.**

4. **Click Compressed (Zipped) Folder.** File Explorer creates the compressed folder and adds the selected files to it. (The new compressed folder is named after whichever of the selected files you right-clicked. Feel free to rename the compressed folder as needed.)

Specifying a different app when opening a document

A document's default app appears when you double-click the document. You may have situations where you prefer to open a particular document with an app other than the default. For example, double-clicking a picture file opens it in the Photos app. However, you may prefer to open the picture file in Paint 3D or some other image-editing program so that you can make changes to the picture.

Here are the steps to follow to open any document in an app other than the default:

1. **In File Explorer, open the folder that contains the document you want to open.**

2. **Click the document.**

3. **Click the Home tab.**

4. **In the Open section, use the Open list to click Choose Another App (see Figure 9.15).** When you pull down the Open list, if the app you want to use appears in the list (such as the WordPad app you see in Figure 9.15), you can click the app and skip the remaining steps.

5. **Click More Apps.** Windows displays a full list of the apps you can use to open the document.

6. **Click the app you want to use to open the document.** If the app you want to use doesn't appear in the list, you can click Look for Another App on this PC (it's at the bottom of the list) and then use the Open With dialog box to specify the app.

Click here to display the Open list

| 📄 | 🗐 🗑 ▾ | Documents | | | | | | | | — □ × |

File   Home   Share   View   ^ ❓

📌   📋 📋 ✂ Cut   🔳 📋 ✖ 🖊   🗐 New item ▾   📄 🖥 Open ▾   ⬛ Select all
Pin to Quick   Copy   Paste   📋 Copy path   Move   Copy   Delete Rename   New   📄 Easy   Notepad   ⬛ Select none
access   📋 Paste shortcut   to ▾   to ▾   ▾   folder   WordPad   ⬛ Invert selection

Clipboard   Organize   New   🏪 Search the Microsoft Store   Select

← → ▾ ↑ 📁 > This PC > Documents   ✓ 🔄   Choose another app

⭐ Quick access   📄 Shaggy Dog Story.docx   📄 Technically Speaking.docx   📄 The Jargon of Junk Food.rtf
                       W Microsoft Word Document   W Microsoft Word Document   Rich Text Document
🖥 Desktop   📌   13.5 KB   219 KB   4.47 KB
⬇ Downloads   📌   📄 The Love of Word.docx   📄 To-Do List.txt   📄 Trips v. Vacations.docx
📄 Documents   📌   W Microsoft Word Document   ☑ Text Document   Microsoft Word Document
                       23.4 KB   0 bytes   142 KB

9.15 Pull down the Open list.

Genius

If you want to open every file of the same type—such as Text Document files or Rich Text Format files—in the same program, follow Steps 1 to 6 and then click the Always Use This App to Open *.ext* Files check box, where *.ext* is the file extension of the file type you're working with.

7. **Click OK.** Windows opens the document in the app you chose.

What Are Some Ways to Enhance PC Security?

Sign-in options

Require sign-in

If you've been away, when should Windows require you to sign in again?

When PC wakes up from sleep ⌄

✦🔒 Dynamic lock

Windows can use devices that are paired to your PC to know when you're away and lock your PC when those devices go out of range.

☑ Allow Windows to automatically lock your device when you're away

💻 ——— 📱 Pauls iPhone

Bluetooth & other devices

Learn more

Many experts believe that most security and privacy violations occur not remotely from the Internet, but locally, right at your computer. That is, security and privacy are usually compromised by someone sitting down at a PC while the user isn't around. That makes sense, because having physical access to a computer allows an intruder to install malicious programs, disable security features, and steal sensitive data, such as passwords and financial information. If you're worried about having your security compromised by someone gaining access to your computer, Windows offers a number of tools that you can use to protect your PC.

Enhancing Sign-In Security **190**

Locking Your PC to Prevent Others from Using It **195**

Enhancing Your Privacy..................................... **198**

Enhancing Sign-In Security

Windows security begins when you sign in to your account right after you start your computer. If a would-be intruder or snoop can't get past the sign-in screen, then you've gone a long way to ensuring the security of your system. The next few sections take you through a few methods for bolstering your sign-in security.

Creating a strong password

Sign-in security starts with assigning a password to each user account on the computer. This prevents unauthorized users from accessing the system, and it enables you to lock your computer (as I describe later in this chapter).

However, it's not enough to use just any old password that pops into your head. To ensure the strongest security for your Windows account, you need to make your password robust enough that it's impossible to guess and impervious to software programs designed to try different password combinations. Such a password is called a *strong password*. Ideally, you should build a password that provides maximum protection while still being easy to remember.

Lots of books suggest ridiculously abstruse password schemes (I've written some of those books myself), but you need to know only three things to create strong-like-a-bull passwords:

- **Use passwords that are at least 12 characters long.** Shorter passwords are susceptible to programs that try every letter combination. You can combine the 26 letters of the alphabet into about 12 million 5-letter word combinations, which is no big deal for a fast program. If you use 12-letter passwords—as many experts recommend—the number of combinations goes beyond mind-boggling: 90 quadrillion, or 90,000 trillion!

- **Mix up the character types.** The secret to a strong password is to include characters from the following categories: lowercase letters, uppercase letters, punctuation marks, numbers, and symbols. If you include at least one character from three (or, even better, all five) of these categories, you're well on your way to a strong password.

- **Don't be obvious.** Because forgetting a password is inconvenient, many people use meaningful words or numbers so that their passwords will be easier to remember. Unfortunately, this means that they often use extremely obvious terms, such as their name, the name of a family member or colleague, their birthdate, or their Social Security number. Being this obvious is just asking for trouble. Adding

123 or a punctuation mark (!) to the end of the password doesn't help much, either. Password-cracking programs try those.

- **Create your own password system.** The problem with passwords is that it's impossible to remember them, especially if you use a different password for each account (as you should). To help remember, come up with a system based on a phrase or other text that you modify for each account. For example, let's say you create a system based on the phrase *The7DeadlySins*. Replace the number 7 with the length of the account name, and insert the account's name between Deadly and Sins. For example, your Windows password would be *The7DeadlyWindowsSins*, your Facebook password would be *The8DeadlyFacebookSins*, and so on.

Updating your account password

Once you've come up with a strong password (as I describe in the previous section), follow these steps to update your account password:

1. **Click Start, click your user tile, and then click Change Account Settings.** Windows launches the Settings app and displays the Your Info screen. (An alternative way to get here is to open Settings and click Accounts.)

2. **Click Sign-In Options.**

3. **Click Password.**

4. **Click Change.** Windows asks you to verify that you have access to your account.

5. **Verify your account using one of the following methods:**

   - If you've already configured your account with a PIN (which I show you how to do later in this chapter), enter your PIN.

   - If you haven't set up a PIN yet, enter your account password and then click Sign In.

   Either way, Windows displays the Change Your Password dialog box.

6. **Type your current password.**

7. **Type your new password.**

8. **Click Next.** Windows lets you know that your password has been changed.

9. **Click Finish.** You can use your new password the next time you sign in to Windows.

Creating a picture password

If you are serious about your tablet's security, then you should have configured your Windows user account with a strong password. However, the stronger the password you use, the more cumbersome it is to enter, especially if you're using a touch keyboard.

To making signing in easier, you can switch to a picture password. In this case, your "password" is a series of three gestures—any combination of a tap (or click), a straight line, or a circle—that you apply to a photo. (These gestures are easiest to perform using a touchscreen, but you can also do them with a mouse.) Windows displays the photo at startup, and you repeat your gestures, in order, to sign in to Windows.

Caution

The biggest drawback to using a picture password is that it is possible for a malicious user to view and possibly even record your gestures using a camera. Unlike a regular text password, where the characters appear as dots to prevent someone from seeing them, your gestures have no such protection.

Follow these steps to create a picture password:

1. **Click Start, click your user tile, and then click Change Account Settings.** Windows launches the Settings app and displays the Your Info screen.

2. **Click Sign-In Options.**

3. **Click Picture Password.**

4. **Click Add.** Windows prompts you for your account password.

5. **Type your password and then click OK.** Windows opens the Welcome to Picture Password screen.

6. **Click Choose Picture.** The Open dialog box appears.

7. **Click the picture that you want to use and then click Open.** In the same way that you shouldn't choose a regular account password that's extremely obvious, such as the word *password* or your username, you should take care to avoid creating an obvious picture password. For example, if you were using a photo showing three faces, an obvious picture password would be a click on each face.

8. **Drag the picture so that the image is positioned where you want, and then click Use this Picture.** The Set Up Your Gestures screen appears.

9. **Use your mouse or, on a touchscreen PC, your finger or a stylus, to draw three gestures.** A good picture password not only uses all three available gestures, but also uses them in nonobvious ways. To ensure that you have memorized your picture password, you should sign out of your account a few times and then sign back on using the picture password.

10. **Repeat the gestures to confirm.**

11. **Click Finish.** The next time that you sign in to Windows, you will be prompted to enter your picture password gestures.

If you forget your gestures, you can ask Windows to show them to you. At the sign-in screen, click Sign-In Options and then click the Microsoft Account Password icon to sign in with your regular password. To get a reminder of your picture password gestures, follow Steps 1 through 3 in this section, click Change, type your user account password, and click OK. In the Change Your Picture Password screen, click Replay. Click the picture to see each gesture.

Caution

Your picture password is applied to your user account along with your existing text-based password. That is, the picture password does *not* replace your text password. It's very simple for someone to bypass the picture password and sign in using the text password, so it is vital that you still protect your PC with a strong text password.

Signing in with a PIN

You can make it easier to sign in and you can enhance the security of your PC by using a Windows Hello PIN (personal identification number). A PIN makes it easier to sign in because most PINs use only four digits, which is much faster to type than a strong password that might have a dozen characters, including uppercase and lowercase letters, numbers, and symbols. A PIN enhances the security of your device because the PIN is a device-specific security measure. Unlike a password, which is sent to and stored on a server, your PIN is associated only with your device.

Here are the steps to follow to set up a PIN sign-in for your PC:

1. **Click Start, click your user tile, and then click Change Account Settings.**
   Windows launches the Settings app and displays the Your Info screen.

2. **Click Sign-In Options.**

3. **Click Windows Hello PIN.**

4. **Click Add.** The Create a PIN screen appears.

5. **Click Next.** Windows prompts you for your account password.

6. **Type your password and then click Sign In.** The Set Up a PIN dialog box appears.

7. **Type your PIN twice, as shown in Figure 10.1.** If you want to use letters and symbols in your PIN, you can click the Include Letters and Symbols check box.

10.1 Enter your PIN twice to confirm it.

8. **Click OK.** The next time that you start your PC, you'll be prompted to enter your PIN to sign in.

Note

If you forget your PIN, display the sign-on screen, click Sign-In Options, and then click the Microsoft Account Password icon to sign in with your regular password. Once you're signed in, display the Settings app's Sign-In Options screen, click Windows Hello PIN, and then click I Forgot My PIN.

Setting up a fingerprint sign-in

If your PC comes with a built-in fingerprint reader, or you have an external reader attached to your PC, you can use the Windows Hello feature to teach Windows your fingerprint and use it to sign in. Because your fingerprint is unique, this ensures that only you can access your PC. Also, if you're in a public place, you don't have to enter a password or use picture password gestures that could be observed by a nearby snoop. Follow these steps to set up a fingerprint sign-in:

1. **Click Start, click your user tile, and then click Change Account Settings.** Windows launches the Settings app and displays the Your Info screen.

2. **Click Sign-In Options.**

3. **Click Picture Password.** Note that you need to run this only if you're running Windows on a small screen.

4. **Click Windows Hello Fingerprint and then click Set Up.** The Windows Hello Setup dialog box appears.

5. **Click Get Started.** Windows prompts you for your account PIN.

6. **Type your PIN.** If you don't have a PIN, see the previous section. Windows Hello prompts you to scan your fingerprint.

7. **Briefly place your finger on, and then lift your finger off, your PC's fingerprint reader.** Windows shows the progress of the scan, as shown in Figure 10.2.

8. **Follow the prompts to repeat Step 7 until the scan is complete.**

9. **Click Close.** The next time that you start your PC, you can click Sign-In Options and then click the Fingerprint icon to sign in by placing your finger on the fingerprint reader.

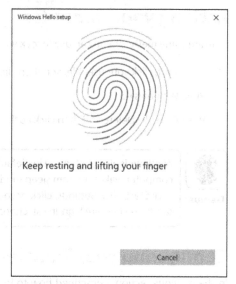

Windows Hello setup ✕

Keep resting and lifting your finger

Cancel

10.2 Windows shows you the progress of the fingerprint scan.

Note that you're free to use as many of your fingerprints as you like. If you still have the final dialog box on-screen, click Add Another Finger. Otherwise, display the Settings app's Sign-In Options screen, click Windows Hello Fingerprint, and then click Add Another.

Locking Your PC to Prevent Others from Using It

Many security measures rely on the fact that you've entered the appropriate password (or another sign-in option such as a PIN) to sign in to your Windows account. In other words, after you sign in, you become a "trusted" user.

But what happens when you leave your desk? If you remain signed in to Windows, any other person who sits down at your computer can take advantage of your trusted-user status to view and work with secure files. You could prevent this by shutting down your computer every time you leave your desk, but that's not very practical. A better solution is to lock your system before leaving your desk. Anyone who tries to use your computer must enter your password (or PIN) to access the Windows desktop.

Locking your computer

Here are some methods you can use to lock your PC:

- Click Start, click your user tile, and then click Lock.
- Press Windows+L.
- Press Ctrl+Alt+Delete and then click Lock.

Genius

Windows is also configured by default to display the logon screen when your computer wakes up from sleep mode. To make sure this setting is activated, click Start, click Settings, click Accounts, and then click the Sign-In Options tab. In the Require Sign-in list, choose When PC Wakes Up from Sleep.

Configuring your PC to lock automatically

In the previous section, I described how to lock your computer to prevent an intruder from accessing your desktop while you are away from your PC. The locking technique is easy enough to do, but the hard part is remembering to do it. If you're late for a meeting or other appointment, locking up your machine is probably the last thing on your mind as you dash out the door. If you later remember that you forgot to lock your computer, you may spend the next while worrying about your PC.

To avoid the worrying and to ensure that some snoop can't access your PC if you forget to lock it, you can configure the Dynamic Lock feature to lock your computer automatically when a connected mobile device, such as your smartphone, is no longer within range of the PC.

Pairing a Bluetooth mobile device

To get started, you first have to connect—or *pair*—a Bluetooth device to your PC. Pairing means your PC and your device automatically connect when they're within 33 feet of each other. For our purposes this also means that your PC and your device automatically *disconnect* when they're more than 33 feet apart, and it's that automatic disconnect that triggers the Dynamic Lock feature.

Follow these steps to pair a mobile device with your Windows PC:

1. **On your mobile device, make sure Bluetooth is turned on.**

2. **On your PC, click Start, then click Settings.** You can also open Settings by pressing Windows+I. The Settings app appears.

3. Click Devices.

4. Click Add Bluetooth or Other Device. The Add a Device screen appears.

5. Click Bluetooth. Windows begins looking for Bluetooth-enabled devices that are within range.

6. When your device appears, click it. Windows initiates the connection by displaying a PIN (see Figure 10.3) that also appears on your mobile device.

7. Check that this PIN is the same as the PIN displayed on your mobile device. In most cases, you also have to tap Pair on the device.

8. Click Connect. Windows pairs with your device.

9. Click Done. You can now set up Dynamic Lock with the paired mobile device.

PIN

10.3 Windows displays a PIN that should match what you see on your mobile device.

Activating Dynamic Lock

With a mobile device paired with your PC via Bluetooth, follow these steps to activate the Dynamic Lock feature:

1. **Click Start, click your user tile, and then click Change Account Settings.**
   Windows launches the Settings app and displays the Your Info screen.

2. **Click Sign-In Options.**

3. **Click the Allow Windows to Automatically Lock Your Device When You're Away check box, as shown in Figure 10.4.** Windows now automatically locks your PC when you take your mobile device more than 33 feet away from your PC.

10.4 Activate the Dynamic Lock feature to automatically lock your PC when your paired mobile device is no longer within range.

Enhancing Your Privacy

Keeping your data safe from theft is vital, but it's just as important to keep your data and your activities safe from prying eyes. What you create, write, and do using your computer is your business, so keeping those things private is paramount. Fortunately, as the next few sections show, Windows comes with quite a few useful tools for enhancing privacy.

Making the Start menu more private

The Start menu is a crucial feature for getting things done with Windows, but it can also betray lots of your secrets. For example, Start can show:

- Which apps you've installed recently
- Which apps you use most often
- Which app items (such as documents or websites) you've opened recently

Unless you actually need these features, it's probably best to turn them off. Here's how it's done:

1. **Click Start and then click Settings.** Windows opens the Settings app.

2. **Click Personalization.**

3. **Click Start.** The Start settings appear.

4. **Click each of the following switches to Off:**

   - Show Recently Added Apps

   - Show Most Used Apps

   - Show Recently Opened Items in Jump Lists on Start. . .

Controlling your private information

By default, Windows enables apps to access many aspects of your system, such as the camera, microphone, and internal antennas such as Wi-Fi and Bluetooth. Windows also enables apps to access personal information such as your location, account information, contacts, and calendar. This access improves your app experience in most cases, but you might be uncomfortable sharing so much with apps, particularly third-party apps. In that case, you can turn off access to your system resources and to your private information, either globally or just for specific apps. Here are the steps to follow:

1. **Click Start and then click Settings.** The Settings app appears.

2. **Click Privacy.** The Privacy settings appear.

3. **Click Location.** The Location settings appear.

4. **Click the Allow Apps to Access Your Location switch to Off, as shown in Figure 10.5.** This prevents apps from using your location.

5. **To remove all location information from your PC, scroll down to the Location History section and click Clear.** Windows removes all your location information.

6. **For each resource that you no longer want to allow apps to access, click the appropriate resource tab.** For example, Figure 10.6 shows a partial listing of the privacy settings for the Camera resource.

Allow apps to access your location

If you allow access, you can use the settings on this page to choose which apps can access your device's precise location and location history to enable location-based experiences such as directions and weather. If you are signed in with a Microsoft account on this device, your last known location is saved to the cloud, and shared with other devices where you are signed in with your Microsoft account. Denying access only blocks the apps listed on this page from accessing your location.

Off

10.5 Turn the Allow Apps to Access Your Location switch Off to prevent app access to your location across all your apps.

← Settings

⌂ Home

Find a setting

Privacy

Windows permissions

App permissions

Location

Camera

Microphone

Voice activation

Notifications

Account info

Contacts

Calendar

Phone calls

Camera

Allow apps to access your camera

If you allow access, you can choose which apps can access your camera by using the settings on this page. Denying access blocks apps from accessing your camera. It does not block Windows Hello.

On

Some desktop apps may still be able to access your camera when settings on this page are off. Find out why

Choose which Microsoft Store apps can access your camera

Turning off an app prevents it from directly accessing your camera. It does not prevent the app from accessing the camera indirectly through the Windows' Camera app. To prevent apps from also accessing the camera indirectly using the Windows' Camera app, you must also turn off access to the Camera app in the following list.

Sort by: Name ∨

3D Viewer — On

Camera — On
Last accessed 2/6/2020 2:48:58 PM

Desktop App Web Viewer — Off

10.6 Some of the privacy settings associated with the Camera resource.

7. **Click the switch that controls global access to Off.** For example, to prevent apps from using your PC's camera, click the Allow Apps to Access Your Camera switch to Off. Alternatively, you can use the app-specific switches to turn off access for individual apps.

Stopping an app's notifications

If an app's notifications contain private information, you can turn them off by following these steps:

1. **Click Start and then click Settings.** The Settings app appears.

2. **Click System.** The System settings appear.

3. **Click Notifications & Actions.** The Notifications & Actions settings appear.

4. **In the Get Notifications from These Senders section, for each app that you want notifications disabled, click the switch to Off, as shown in Figure 10.7.**

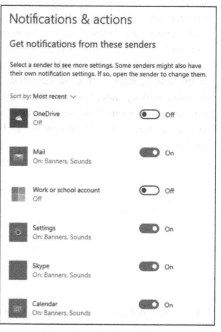

Notifications & actions

Get notifications from these senders

Select a sender to see more settings. Some senders might also have their own notification settings. If so, open the sender to change them.

Sort by: Most recent ∨

OneDrive
Off — Off

Mail
On: Banners, Sounds — On

Work or school account
Off — Off

Settings
On: Banners, Sounds — On

Skype
On: Banners, Sounds — On

Calendar
On: Banners, Sounds — On

Clearing your activity history

As you use your computer, Windows keeps track of various activities you perform: the apps you use, the

10.7 Click an app's switch to Off to prevent the app from displaying notifications.

documents you open, and the websites you visit. This activity is easily accessible by clicking Task View in the taskbar. That's certainly convenient, but it also means that other people who have access to your PC can also easily view your recent activities. To avoid this privacy violation, you can tell Windows to clear all your recent activities. Optionally, you can also configure Windows to not track your activities at all. Follow these steps:

1. **Click Start and then click Settings.** The Settings app appears.

2. **Click Privacy.** The Privacy settings appear.

3. **Click Activity History.** The Activity History settings appear.

4. **To remove all activity history from your PC, scroll down to the Clear Activity History section and click Clear.** Windows removes all your activity history.

5. **If you don't want Windows to track your activities, clear the Store My Activity History on this Device check box, as shown in Figure 10.8.** Windows stops tracking your activity.

Clearing Other Activity

Via your Microsoft account, Microsoft also tracks your web browsing history, search history, location activity, Cortana voice activity, media activity, which Microsoft products and services you use, performance and reliability data for those products and services, data Cortana stores about you, and your LinkedIn data. To clear some or all of this activity, follow Steps 1 to 3 in this section, and then click Manage My Microsoft Account Activity Data. Microsoft Edge appears and takes you to Microsoft's main Privacy portal. From there, you can view and clear your activity in any of the nine tracked categories mentioned previously by clicking that category's View and Clear button.

Activity history

Jump back into what you were doing on your device by storing your activity history, including info about websites you browse and how you use apps and services.

☐ Store my activity history on this device

10.8 You can configure Windows to no longer track your activity.

Resetting your computer to preserve privacy

As you use your computer, you accumulate a large amount of personal data: documents, installed apps, Microsoft Edge favorites, email messages, photos, and much more. If you're selling your computer or giving it away, you probably don't want the recipient to have access to all that personal data. To prevent this, you can reset the computer, which deletes all your personal data and reinstalls a fresh copy of Windows.

Follow these steps to reset your PC:

1. **Click Start and then click Settings.** The Settings app appears.

2. **Click Update & Security.** The Update & Security settings appear.

3. **Click Recovery.** The Recovery settings appear.

4. **Under Reset this PC, click Get Started.** The User Account Control dialog box appears so that you can verify that you want to reset your PC.

5. **Enter the password or PIN of your PC's administrator account.** Reset this PC asks how you want to remove your personal files, as shown in Figure 10.9.

Reset this PC

Choose an option

Keep my files
Removes apps and settings, but keeps your personal files.

Remove everything
Removes all of your personal files, apps, and settings.

Help me choose   Cancel

10.9 If you're selling or donating your PC, you'll want to remove everything.

Genius

The Keep My Files option deletes your apps and your Windows settings, but it leaves your files on your PC, so this isn't the option you want if you're giving away or selling your PC. Instead, you want the Remove Everything option, which not only removes your apps and your custom Windows settings, but it also removes all your personal files.

6. **Click Remove Everything.** Reset this PC asks how you want to reinstall Windows.

7. **Click Cloud Download.** This is the faster option, but it requires at least 4GB of free hard drive space. If your PC's hard drive doesn't have that much free space (to learn how to check this, see Chapter 12), click Local Reinstall, instead. Reset this PC displays the Additional Settings dialog box.

8. **(Optional) If you have very sensitive or confidential data on your PC, click Change Settings, click the Clean Data? switch to On, and then click Confirm.** This tells Reset this PC to ensure that any data you've stored on your computer can't be recovered using special tools. This process takes longer, but it gives you the highest privacy.

9. **Click Next.** The Ready to Reset this PC screen appears.

10. **Click Reset.** Windows resets your computer.

How Do I Increase Internet Privacy and Security?

Tracking prevention ⓘ

Websites use trackers to collect info about your browsing. Websites may use this info to improve sites and show you content like personalized ads. Some trackers collect and send your info to sites you haven't visited.

Tracking prevention ●

Basic	Balanced (Recommended)	Strict
• Allows most trackers across all sites	• Blocks trackers from sites you haven't visited	• Blocks a majority of trackers from all sites
• Content and ads will likely be personalized	• Content and ads will likely be less personalized	• Content and ads will likely have minimal personalization
• Sites will work as expected	• Sites will work as expected	• Parts of sites might not work
• Blocks known harmful trackers	• Blocks known harmful trackers	• Blocks known harmful trackers

Blocked trackers >
View the sites that we've blocked from tracking you

Exceptions >
Allow all trackers on sites you choose

Always use "Strict" tracking prevention when browsing InPrivate ●

The Internet is one of the world's great resources, but it has lured more than a few malicious hackers, system intruders, and con artists of every stripe. These miscreants spend their waking hours thinking up ways to disrupt the Internet, break into your online computer, and steal everything from your credit card numbers to your full identity. As newspaper headlines attest almost daily, cybercrime is a big business, so it pays to play it safe. This chapter helps by offering you a full suite of tasks and techniques designed to make your web and email tasks as safe as possible.

Making the Web More Secure **206**

Making the Web More Private **209**

Enhancing Email Security and Privacy **215**

Making the Web More Secure

The web is a wonder, but it would be a mistake to think of the web as a kind of digital Shangri-La where bad things never happen to good people. The web is a reflection of life, and as such it can also reflect the bad side. So, unfortunately, the web is home to people who'd like to take over your computer, steal your credit card data, grab your online banking password, and generally just cause whatever mischief and mayhem they think they can get away with. Fortunately, these digital ne'er-do-wells are relatively rare, so it's not like you're going to be constantly accosted as you travel around the web. But e-hooligans do exist, so the prudent web surfer understands the potential threats and takes steps to prevent bad things from happening. This section tells you everything you need to know to stay safe when you're on the web.

Avoiding viruses

A *virus* is a malevolent program that installs itself on your PC without your permission. After it's done that, the virus might then steal your data, record your passwords, trash your files, or turn your PC into a zombie computer that the virus forces into attacking other PCs. Viruses are nasty bits of business no matter how you slice it, so they're to be avoided like the plague that they are.

The best way to inoculate your PC against virus infections is to use an antivirus program. This special software application is designed to detect, block, and if necessary, remove viruses. The good news is that your Windows PC already comes with an antivirus program called Windows Defender. However, having an antivirus program installed is a good (and necessary) thing, but it doesn't mean you can let your guard down while you surf the web. You should avoid tempting fate by following these simple precautions:

- **Look for—but do *not* click—links to programs or scripts.** Some nasty websites attempt to install a virus by setting up an innocuous-looking link that actually connects you to a program or script that installs a virus on your PC. To be safe, point at each link before you click it and take a look at the address displayed in the bottom-left corner of the Edge window. Don't click the link if the address isn't what you're expecting (for example, you see http://x4z9arb.com instead of http://amazon.com) or if the filename ends with any of the following extensions: .bat, .cmd, .com, .doc, .exe, .js, .ppt, .reg, .vb, .vbs, .wsh, or .xls.

- **Avoid downloading files from websites that you don't know or trust.** Downloading files from the web to your PC is a common task and one that you generally don't have to worry about because files from reputable websites are almost certainly virus-free. However, if you're using a website that you don't know or don't trust, it's probably best to avoid the download altogether. If you need the file, be sure to use Windows Defender to scan the file for infection before opening it.

Genius

To scan a downloaded file, use File Explorer to open the Downloads folder, right-click the downloaded file, and then click Scan with Microsoft Defender.

● **Ignore online ads that make wild or too-good-to-be-true claims.** As you surf the web, you'll come across sites that display ads claiming that "you have messages waiting" or that "you've won a prize." Believe me, you have no messages and you haven't won anything. Most of these ads are just annoying come-ons (often called "clickbait"), but some of them have a hidden virus payload that activates when you click the ad.

Caution

The main ads to avoid are those that display realistic looking "dialog boxes" that tell you "Your PC Is Infected" or "Potential Threats Detected" and offer a button that you're urged to click to solve the problem. Don't do it! The most likely scenario is that you'll trigger a virus installation that really will leave your PC infected!

● **Don't allow pop-up windows.** A *pop-up window* is a web page that appears in a separate browser window. Some sites use pop-ups for activities such as logging in, but this is relatively rare nowadays. Most pop-ups are just intrusive advertisements, but some are more nefarious and will trigger a virus download if you click anything within the pop-up. Microsoft Edge is aware of all this, and it automatically blocks pop-ups when it detects them. You'll know when this is happening because you'll see the Pop-ups Were Blocked on this Page icon on the right side of the Address bar, as shown in Figure 11.1.

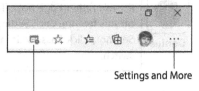

Settings and More

Pop-ups Were Blocked on this Page

11.1 Edge displays the Pop-ups Were Blocked on this Page icon when it blocks one or more pop-up windows.

Genius

What if you *do* want to see a pop-up for a particular site? In that case, click the Pop-ups Were Blocked on this Page icon, click the Always Allow Pop-ups and Redirects from *address* radio button (where *address* is the address of the current page), and then click Done.

Opting to never save a site's password

When you sign in to a website where you have an account, you normally enter your account's username and password. After you do that, Edge usually displays a Save Password dialog box like the one shown in Figure 11.2. If you click Save, Edge saves your account data and automatically fills in the username and password the next time you sign in to the site.

Edge is very secure, so it's fine to click Save. If you'd rather not save your password, click Close (X) to move on with your life. However, there are certain sites where you should *never* save your password. These sites include online banking pages, online investment accounts, and any other site where signing in gives access to sensitive, secure, or private data. For those sites, you should click Never in the Save Password dialog box, which tells Edge to never ask you again about saving the password for the site.

Save password ✕

Microsoft Edge will save and fill your password for this site next time.

4545454545454545 ⌄

•••••••••••• ⌄ 👁

Save · Never

11.2 When you sign in to a site, Edge displays the Save Password dialog box to ask if you want to save the account username and password.

Genius | If you'd rather Edge not offer to save passwords for *any* site, you can turn off this feature. Click Settings and More (pointed out in Figure 11.1), click Settings, click Passwords, and then turn off the Offer to Save Passwords switch.

Deleting a saved website password

If you click Save in the Save Password dialog box (see Figure 11.2) and then access the site's sign-in page at a later date, Edge fills in the password for you automatically. This is convenient, to be sure, but it has a downside: Anyone who uses your computer can also access the password-protected content. If you've saved a password for a site and you no longer feel comfortable having the saved password on your computer, you can follow these steps to delete the saved password from Edge:

1. **Click Settings and More.** I pointed out this icon in Figure 11.1.

2. **Click Settings.** Edge opens the Settings tab.

3. **Click Passwords.** Edge opens the Passwords page.

4. **To the right of the password you want to delete, click More Actions (see Figure 11.3), and then click Delete.** Edge deletes the saved password.

← ○ ⌂ ● Edge | edge://settings/passwords	☆ ☆ ⊕ ● ⋯

≡ Settings

🔍 Search settings

← Profiles / Passwords

🔍 Search passwords

Offer to save passwords

Sign in automatically
If this is turned off, we'll ask you for permission every time before signing in to a website

Saved passwords

⋯

Website	Username	Password		
cibconline.cibc.com	4545454545454545	••••••••••	👁 ⋯	📋 Details
accounts.google.com	paul@logophilialtd.com	••••••••••	👁 ⋯	🗑 Delete ⟍

More Actions

Show Password

11.3 Click the site's More Actions icon and then click Delete.

Genius

If you've forgotten a site's password and you opted to save it earlier, open the Passwords tab, click the site's Show Password icon (the eye; see Figure 11.3), then enter the PIN or password for your Windows account.

Making the Web More Private

Even if you never come across an online scam or a site that attempts to install a virus on your PC, there are still lots of other threats that revolve more around keeping your browsing data and activities private. The next few sections offer a few tools and techniques for keeping your browsing info to yourself.

Deleting your browsing data to ensure privacy

As you visit websites, Edge maintains information about the sites you visit. Edge also stores—or *caches*—copies of page text, images, and other content so that sites load faster the next time you view them. Similarly, Edge also saves the names of files you have downloaded as well as text and passwords that you have typed into forms. Edge also maintains *cookies*, which are small text files that store information such as site preferences and site logon data.

Saving all this data is useful because it enables you to quickly revisit a site. However, it's also dangerous because other people who use your computer can just as easily visit or view information about those sites. This can be a problem if you visit financial sites, private corporate sites, or some other page that you would not want another person to visit. You reduce this risk by deleting some or all of your browsing history. Here are the steps to follow:

1. **Click Settings and More.** I pointed out this icon in Figure 11.1.

2. **Click Settings.** Edge opens the Settings tab.

3. **Click Menu and then click Privacy and Services.** Edge opens the Privacy page.

4. **In the Clear Browsing Data section, click Choose What to Clear.** Edge displays the Clear Browsing Data dialog box, shown in Figure 11.4. You can also display this dialog box by pressing Ctrl+Shift+Delete.

5. **Use the Time Range list to choose how far back in time you want the browsing data deleted.**

6. **To delete the list of websites you have visited, choose Browsing History.**

Clear browsing data ×

Time range

Last hour ∨

✓ Browsing history
   10 items. Includes autocompletions in the address bar.
✓ Download history
   None
✓ Cookies and other site data
   From 19 sites. Signs you out of most sites.
✓ Cached images and files
   Frees up less than 319 MB. Some sites may load more slowly on your next visit.

This will clear your data across all your synced devices signed in to logophilia@outlook.com. To clear browsing data from this device only, turn off sync.

Clear now   Cancel

11.4 Use the Clear Browsing Data dialog box to clear some or all of your browsing data.

7. **To delete the list of files that you have downloaded, choose Download History.**

8. **To delete cookie files and website data, choose Cookies and Other Site Data.**

9. **To delete saved web page files, choose Cached Images and Files.**

10. **To delete saved passwords, choose Passwords.**

11. **To delete saved form data, choose Autofill Form Data.**

12. **Click Clear Now.** Edge deletes the browsing data you selected.

Genius

If you regularly delete browsing data, following the steps in this section each time can become tiresome. Fortunately, you can configure Edge to make this chore automatic. Follow Steps 1 through 3, then click Choose What to Clear Every Time You Close the Browser. Click the switch to On for each type of data you want Edge to clear automatically every time you close the app.

Turning on private browsing

Edge saves a great deal of data as your surf the web. This data includes temporary Internet files, website data, cookies, surfing history, downloads, form data, and site passwords. If you regularly visit private websites or websites that contain sensitive or secret data, you can ensure that no one else sees any data for these sites by deleting your browsing history, as I describe in the previous section.

However, if these sites represent only a small percentage of the places you visit on the web, deleting your entire browsing history is overkill. A better solution is to turn on Edge's InPrivate browsing feature before you visit private sites. This tells Edge to temporarily stop saving any browsing history. When you're ready to surf regular websites again, you can turn off InPrivate browsing to resume saving your browsing history.

There are two ways to activate InPrivate browsing:

- Click Settings and More (see Figure 11.1) and then click New InPrivate Window.

- Press Ctrl+Shift+N.

Preventing ad sites from tracking you online

As mentioned, a *cookie* is a small text file that's stored on your computer by a website that needs to "remember" information about your session at that site: shopping cart data, page customizations, usernames, passwords, and so on.

No other site can access your cookies, so they're generally safe and private under most—but definitely not all—circumstances. To understand why cookies can sometimes compromise your privacy, you have to understand the difference between the two main cookie types:

- A *first-party cookie* is a cookie set by the website you're viewing.

- A *third-party cookie* is a cookie set by a site other than the one you're viewing.

An ad site might store information about you in a third-party cookie and then use that cookie to track your online movements and activities. The advertiser can do this because it might have an ad on dozens or hundreds of websites, and that ad is the mechanism that enables the site to set and read their cookies.

To prevent this, you can configure Edge to block third-party cookies:

1. **Click Settings and More.** I pointed out this icon in Figure 11.1.

2. **Click Settings.** Edge opens the Settings tab.

3. **Click Menu and then click Site Permissions.** Edge opens the Site Permissions page.

4. **Click Cookies and Site Data.** Edge displays the Cookies and Site Data page.

5. **Click the Block Third-Party Cookies switch to On, as shown in Figure 11.5.** Edge no longer accepts cookies from third-party sites.

☰ Settings	🔎 Search settings
← Site permissions / Cookies and site data	
Allow sites to save and read cookie data (recommended)	⬤
Block third-party cookies When on, sites can't use cookies that track you across the web. Features on some sites may break.	⬤

11.5 Click the Block Third-Party Cookies switch to On to prevent advertisers from tracking you online.

Caution

You might find that disabling third-party cookies causes some websites to load improperly or not at all. This usually means that the site requires information from a third party, but that information cannot get through because the third party cannot set a cookie. In that case, you might be better offer returning Edge to allowing third-party cookies.

Enabling strict tracking prevention

Blocking third-party cookies, as I describe in the previous section, is a useful starting point for preventing your online activities from being tracked. However, the sites you visit might also use other types of content from third-party sites, such as maps, web analytical tools, and, of course, advertisements. Most of this content is benign, but some of it could give a third party access to some of your personal data.

To prevent this, Edge implements *tracking prevention*, which is the web equivalent of a "Do Not Call" list for telephone solicitors. If you block third-party content—that is, you configure that content with a kind of "Do Not Track" label—then Edge prevents any site from requesting that content from the third party. Edge offers three types of tracking prevention:

- **Basic.** Allows most third-party trackers (Edge blocks all trackers that are known to be malicious).

- **Balanced.** Blocks trackers from sites that you've never visited.

- **Strict.** Blocks most third-party trackers.

By default, Edge uses the Balanced tracking prevention, which should work fine for most people. However, if you really don't want to be tracked online, then you can follow these steps to switch to Strict tracking prevention:

1. **Click Settings and More.** I pointed out this icon in Figure 11.1.

2. **Click Settings.** Edge opens the Settings tab.

3. **Click Menu and then click Privacy and Services.** Edge opens the Privacy page.

4. **In the Tracking Prevention section, click Strict, as shown in Figure 11.6.** Edge now blocks most third-party trackers.

11.6 Click Strict to maximize tracking prevention.

Preventing sites from requesting your location

If you have a computer, particularly a tablet PC, that has a built-in Global Positioning System (GPS) receiver, it can pinpoint your location to within a few feet. Even if you have a basic PC that doesn't include GPS technology but does include Wi-Fi, a website can still get a fix on your current location by examining the known wireless access points in your surrounding area.

This all means that it's possible for websites to determine your current location. For example, if you ask Google maps for directions to an address, it defaults to using your current location as the starting point. When this happens, Edge asks you to give permission to the site to track your location (see Figure 11.7). You can then click Block to deny the request.

www.google.com wants to

Know your location

Allow   Block

11.7 Edge asks you for permission to allow a site to determine your location.

If you'd rather not have any websites tracking your location, you can disable this feature by following these steps:

1. **Click Settings and More.** I pointed out this icon in Figure 11.1.

2. **Click Settings.** Edge opens the Settings tab.

3. **Click Menu (if you're running Edge on a small screen) and then click Site Permissions.** Edge opens the Site Permissions page.

4. **Click Location.** Edge displays the Location page.

5. **Click the Ask Before Accessing switch to Off, as shown in Figure 11.8.** Edge now blocks all requests to determine your location.

≡ **Settings**

Search settings

← Site permissions / Location

Ask before accessing (recommended)
Will block if turned off

Block
No sites available

Allow
https://us.flow.microsoft.com:443
embedded on https://us.flow.microsoft.com

Remove

11.8 Click the Ask Before Accessing switch to Off to block all websites from determining your location.

Note

You can also clear any sites that you've previously allowed to access your location. Follow Steps 1 through 4, then click the Remove icon (the trash can pointed out in Figure 11.8) to the right of the site.

Enhancing Email Security and Privacy

Many people think that email is safer than the web because email is, in a sense, "in here" (that is, inside your PC) while the web is "out there" (that is, on the Internet). That would be nice if it were true, but alas it's not. There are plenty of ways that email messages can compromise both security and privacy, so it pays to be cautious with your Inbox.

Avoiding viruses in email

Although malicious websites are a common cause of virus infections, in recent years the most productive method for viruses to replicate has been the humble email message. The virus arrives as a message attachment, usually from someone you know. When you open the attachment, the virus infects your computer and then, without your knowledge, uses your email program and your address book to ship out messages with more copies of itself attached. The nastier versions also mess with your computer by deleting data, corrupting files, or encrypting your files and asking for money to decrypt them (a nasty bit of graft known as a *ransomware attack*).

You can avoid infection from one of these viruses by implementing a few commonsense procedures:

- **Never open an attachment that comes from someone you don't know.**

- **Even if you know the sender, check the message.** If it's vague or extremely short (or just doesn't sound like the sender), you should be immediately suspicious about the attachment. Otherwise, if the attachment isn't something you're expecting, assume that the sender's system is infected. Write back and confirm that the sender emailed the message.

- **Some viruses come packaged as scripts hidden within messages that use the HTML format (the same format that underlies most web pages).** This means that the virus can run just by the message being viewed! If a message looks suspicious, don't open it; just delete it.

To delete a message without clicking it, hover the mouse pointer over the message and then click the Delete This Item icon (the trash can) that appears.

Preventing messages from opening automatically

I mention in the previous section that some viruses can be installed just by viewing a message. If you see a suspicious message, you should delete it without ever clicking on it. However, Mail is set up by default to automatically open a message in the Reading pane if you either move or delete the message above it. That's dangerous behavior, so follow these steps to turn it off:

1. **Click Settings.** This is the gear icon that appears in the lower-left corner of the Mail window. The Settings pane appears.

2. **Click Reading pane.** The Reading Pane settings appear.

3. **Click the Auto-Open Next Item switch to Off.**

4. **Click outside the Settings pane.** Mail puts your new setting into effect.

Thwarting web bugs by blocking images in messages

A *web bug* is a small and usually invisible image, the code for which is inserted into an email message. That code specifies a remote address from which to download the web bug image when you open or preview the message. However, the code also includes a reference to your email address. The remote server makes note of the fact that you received the message, which means your address is a working one and is therefore a good target for further spam messages. By blocking web bugs, you undermine this confirmation and so receive less spam.

Here are the steps to follow to configure Mail not to show images in messages:

1. **Click Settings.** This is the gear icon that appears in the lower-left corner of the Mail window. The Settings pane appears.

2. **Click Reading pane.** The Reading Pane settings appear.

3. **If you have multiple accounts added to Mail, use the External Content section's Select an Account list to choose which account you want to work with.** Alternatively, if you want your new settings to apply to every account you've added to Mail, click the Apply to All Accounts check box.

4. **Click the Automatically Download External Images and Style Formats Except S/MIME Mail switch to Off, as shown in Figure 11.9.**

5. **Click the Automatically Download External Images and Style Formats for S/MIME Mail switch to Off.** Note that this switch is off by default, so you can usually skip this step.

6. **Click outside the Settings pane.** Mail puts your new Reading pane settings into effect.

External content

Select an account

Outlook ⌄

☐ Apply to all accounts

Automatically download external images and style formats except S/MIME Mail

◉ Off

Automatically download external images and style formats for S/MIME Mail

◉ Off

11.9 To prevent Mail from showing images in messages, make sure both External Content switches are set to Off.

Genius

To see the images in a legitimate email message, scroll to the bottom of the message and then click Download Message and Pictures.

Avoiding phishing scams

Phishing refers to creating a replica of an existing web page or using false emails to fool you into submitting personal information, financial data, or a password. It's a whimsical word for a serious bit of business, but the term comes from the fact that Internet scammers are using increasingly sophisticated lures as they "fish" for your sensitive data.

The most common ploy is to copy the web page code from a major site—such as a bank or eBay—and use that code to set up a replica page that appears to be part of the company's site. You receive a fake email with a link to this page, which solicits your credit card data or password. When you submit the form, it sends the data to the scammer while leaving you on an actual page from the company's site so you don't suspect a thing.

A phishing message is a junk email message that appears to come from a legitimate organization, such as a bank, a major retailer, or an Internet service provider (ISP). The message asks you to update your information or warns you that your account is about to expire. In most cases, the message offers a link to a bogus website that tries to fool you into revealing sensitive or private data.

Caution

Never trust any email message or website that asks you to update or confirm sensitive data, such as your bank account number, credit card information, Social Security number, or account password. It's important to remember that no legitimate company or organization will ever contact you via email to update or confirm such information online.

A phishing scammer can easily craft an email message that looks like it came from a legitimate organization. However, there are ways to recognize a phishing message:

- If the message is addressed to an individual but you see something like "Undisclosed recipients" in the To line, you know something's wrong right off the bat.

- The message appears to come from a major corporation or organization, but the text contains numerous spelling and grammatical errors—or even misspells the name of the company!

- Position the mouse pointer over any links in the message and examine the address that appears in the status bar. If the address is clearly one that's not associated with the company, the message is almost certainly a phishing attempt.

How Do I Maintain Windows?

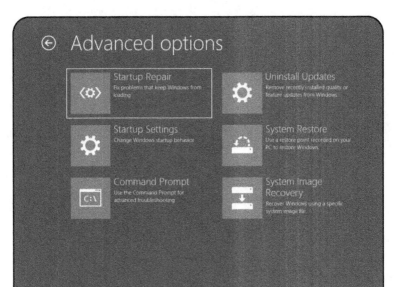

Computer problems, like the proverbial death and taxes, are a constant in life. Whether it's a hard drive failure, a power outage that destroys files, or a virus that invades your system, the issue isn't *whether* something will go wrong, but rather *when* it will happen. Instead of waiting to deal with difficulties after they've occurred, you can become proactive and maintain your system in advance. This reduces the chances that something will go wrong, and it sets up your system for easier recovery from any problems that occur. This chapter shows you various tools and techniques that can help.

Performing a Few Maintenance Chores **222**

Safeguarding Your Files **226**

Using the Windows Recovery Environment **229**

Working with a Recovery Drive **233**

Working with Restore Points **235**

Performing a Few Maintenance Chores

To keep your system running smoothly, maintain top performance, and reduce the risk of computer problems, you need to perform some routine maintenance chores. That's what this whole chapter is about, really, but in this section you learn a few useful maintenance tasks to get you started.

Scheduling automatic maintenance

When you set up Windows, you might have been asked to choose how you wanted to handle the periodic updates that Microsoft makes available for bug fixes, security enhancements, and updated features. If you chose the option to have the updates installed automatically, then Windows automatically checks for, downloads, and installs updates during the *maintenance window*, which is defined by default as follows:

- Maintenance is performed each day at 2:00 a.m.

- If you're using your computer, maintenance is postponed until you're no longer using it.

- If your computer is in sleep mode, maintenance is postponed until the computer is awake.

- If the maintenance server is running late, maintenance is postponed until the server is ready, as long as your computer is not being used and is awake.

Windows uses the maintenance window not only to check for updates, but also to run Windows Defender security scans and to perform system diagnostics. If the default 2:00 a.m. window is inconvenient for you, you can configure the maintenance window to a time more suited to your own schedule:

1. **In the taskbar's Search box, type** main. That should be enough to see Change Automatic Maintenance Settings in the search results. If not, keep typing the rest of the word "maintenance" until you see that result.

2. **Click Change Automatic Maintenance Settings.** The Automatic Maintenance window appears, as shown in Figure 12.1.

3. **Use the Run Maintenance Tasks Daily At list to select the time you want to use as the basis of the maintenance window.**

4. **Click OK.** Windows now uses the new time as the start of the maintenance window.

Don't Miss Maintenance

One of the major causes of missing a maintenance window is having your computer asleep when the window arrives. By default, Windows waits until the PC is awake again to start the maintenance window, but by then you're likely using the computer, so maintenance is delayed yet again.

To avoid this, configure Windows to wake your computer when the maintenance window arrives. Note, however, that Windows will only wake your notebook or tablet if it's not running on batteries. Follow Steps 1 and 2 to open the Automatic Maintenance window, and then click the Allow Scheduled Maintenance to Wake Up My Computer at the Scheduled Time check box. Click OK to put the new setting into effect.

12.1 Use the Automatic Maintenance window to schedule when Windows performs automatic maintenance.

Checking hard drive free space

To ensure that your PC's hard drive doesn't become full, you should periodically check how much free space it has left. This is important because if you run out of room on your hard drive, you can't install more programs or create more documents, and your PC's performance will suffer.

Of particular concern is the hard drive on which Windows is installed, usually drive C. If this hard drive's free space becomes low—say, less than about 20 or 25GB—Windows runs slowly. With normal computer use, you should check your hard drive free space about once a month.

Note

You can also check the free space on a memory card or flash drive. Before you continue, insert the card or drive into the appropriate slot or port on your PC.

Follow these steps to check how much free space is left on a hard drive:

1. **Open File Explorer.** You can either click the File Explorer icon on the taskbar or click Start and then click either Documents or Pictures.

2. **Click This PC.** The This PC folder appears.

3. **Examine the tile of the drive you want to check.** The amount of free space on the drive is specified as part of the drive's tile data, as pointed out in Figure 12.2. Note, too, that if a drive's free space is dangerously low, the bar that indicates how much disk space the drive is using (also pointed out in Figure 12.2) will appear as red.

Note

If you don't see the tiles, click the View tab and then click Tiles.

Dealing with Low Hard Drive Free Space

If your hard drive space is becoming low, you can do three things:

- **Delete or move personal files.** If you have personal files—particularly large media files such as images, music, and videos—that you no longer need, either delete them or move them to a backup drive.

- **Remove apps.** If you have apps that you no longer use, uninstall them. (To uninstall most apps, click Start, right-click the app, and then click Uninstall. When Windows asks you to confirm, click Uninstall.)

- **Run Disk Cleanup.** Use the Storage feature to delete files that Windows no longer uses. See the next section.

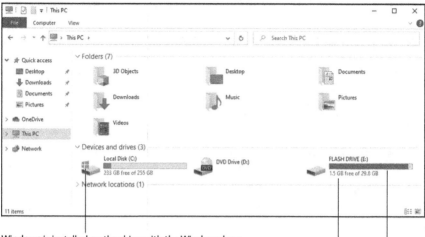

Windows is installed on the drive with the Windows logo

This value tells you the amount of free space on the drive

This bar gives you a visual indication of how much disk space the drive is using

12.2 Use the This PC window to read and see how much free space is left on a drive.

Deleting unnecessary files

Today's hard drives are quite large, with capacities measured in the thousands of gigabytes (or terabytes). However, the expanding capacity of modern hard drives has been offset to a certain extent by the expanding amount of data that we store on those drives. This is partially due to the increasing size of many software programs. However, it's mostly caused by extremely large media files (such as digital movies and TV shows) and extremely large collections of smaller media files (particularly digital music and photos), all of which can take up a lot of space on a hard drive. This means that even with hard drive capacities measured in terabytes, it's still possible to run low on storage space.

Therefore, you should run the Storage feature whenever your Windows hard drive free space becomes too low, particularly less than about 25GB. To open Storage, type **storage** in the taskbar's Search box, then click Storage Settings in the search results. The Storage feature gives you three methods for getting rid of unneeded files on the Windows hard drive:

- **Deleting unneeded files automatically.** Click Configure Storage Sense or Run it Now. In the window that appears (see Figure 12.3), click the Storage Sense switch to On. By default, Storage Sense only runs when your Windows hard drive gets low on free space. You can also use the Run Storage Sense list to select an interval when Storage Sense runs (such as Every Week or Every Month). If you want to run Storage Sense right away, click the Clean Now button.

225

← Settings

⌂ Configure Storage Sense or run it now

Storage Sense

◉ On

Storage Sense runs when disk space is low. We clean up enough space
to help your system run its best. We cleaned up 0 bytes of space in the
past month.

Run Storage Sense

During low free disk space (default)   ⌄

Temporary Files

☑ Delete temporary files that my apps aren't using

Delete files in my recycle bin if they have been there for over:

30 days (default)   ⌄

Delete files in my Downloads folder if they haven't been opened for more than:

Never (default)   ⌄

12.3 Use this window to enable, configure, and run the Storage Sense feature.

- **Following cleanup recommendations.** Click See Cleanup Recommendations to display a list of what Windows considers to be unneeded files. Click the check box beside each item you want to delete, then click the Clean Up *Size* button, where *Size* is the amount of drive space you free up by removing the selected items.

- **Deleting unneeded files manually.** Click a category such as Temporary Files or Apps & Features, click the check box beside each item you want to delete, then click Remove Files.

Safeguarding Your Files

Your files are probably your most precious PC resource, so it pays to take a bit of time to ensure your files are safe and sound. The next few sections show you some useful ways to protect your files.

Keeping a history of your files

If you want to keep a particular file safe, perhaps the easiest method is to make a copy of that file on another hard drive or online. However, there may be times when backing up a file just by making a copy isn't good enough. For example, if you make frequent changes to a file, you might want to copy not only the current version, but also the versions from an hour ago, a day ago, a week ago, and so on. In Windows, these previous versions of a file are called its *file history*, and you can save this data for all your documents by activating a feature called File History. Here are the steps to follow:

1. **Connect an external drive to your PC.** The drive should have enough capacity to hold your files, so an external hard drive is probably best. If you see a notification, click it, click Configure this Drive for Backup, and then skip Steps 3 and 4.

2. **In the taskbar's Search box, type** file history.

3. **Click Backup settings.** The Settings app runs and displays the Backup tab.

4. **Click Add a Drive.** The Select a Drive window appears.

5. **Click the drive you want to use for File History.** Windows activates File History and begins saving copies of your files to the external drive.

Restoring a file from your history

If you improperly edit, accidentally delete, or corrupt a file through a system crash, in many cases you can restore a previous version of the file. Why would you want to revert to a previous version of a file? One reason is that you might improperly edit the file by deleting or changing important data. In some cases, you may be able to restore that data by going back to a previous version of the file. Another reason is that the file might become corrupted if the program or Windows crashes. You can get a working version of the file back by restoring a previous version.

If you've been saving file versions using the File History feature (as I describe in the previous section), follow these steps to restore a previous version of a file:

1. **In the taskbar's Search box, type** restore.

2. **Click Restore Your Files with File History.** The Home - File History window appears.

3. **Double-click the library or folder that contains the file you want to restore.**

4. **Open the folder that contains the file.**

5. **Click Previous Version until you open the version of the folder you want to use.**

6. **Click the file you want to restore.**

7. **Click Restore to Original Location.** If the original folder has a file with the same name, File History asks what you want to do.

8. **Select an option:**

   - You can click Replace the File in the Destination to overwrite the existing file with the previous version.

   - You can click Skip this File to do nothing.

   - You can click Compare Info for Both Files to decide which file you prefer to keep.

Creating a system image backup

The worst-case scenario for PC problems is a system crash that renders your hard disk or system files unuseable. Your only recourse in such a case is to start from scratch with either a reformatted hard disk or a new hard disk. This usually means that you have to reinstall Windows and then reinstall and reconfigure all your applications. In other words, you are looking at the better part of a day or, more likely, a few days, to recover your system. However, Windows has a feature that takes most of the pain out of recovering your system. It is called a *system image backup* and is actually a complete backup of your Windows installation. It takes a long time to create a system image (at least several hours, depending on how much stuff you have), but it is worth it for the peace of mind it gives you.

Follow these steps to create a system image backup:

1. **In the taskbar's Search box, type** backup.

2. **Click Backup Settings.** The Backup tab of the Settings app appears.

3. **Click Go to Backup and Restore (Windows 7).** The "Windows 7" here just means that this is the same tool that was used to make system image backups way back in the time of Windows 7. It's still perfectly safe to use. The Backup and Restore (Windows 7) window appears.

4. **Click Create a System Image.** The User Account Control dialog box appears.

5. **Type the PIN or password for your PC's administrator account.** The Create a System Image Wizard appears.

6. **Choose a backup destination:**

   - **On a Hard Disk.** Choose this option to use a disk drive on your computer.

   - **On One or More DVDs.** Choose this option if you want to use DVDs to hold the backup.

- **On a Network Location.** Choose this option if you want to use a shared network folder.

7. **Click Next.** The Which Drives Do You Want to Include in the Backup? screen appears.

8. **Click the check box beside each extra drive you want to add to the backup and then click Next.** Windows asks you to confirm your backup settings.

9. **Click Start Backup.** Windows creates the system image.

Note

When the system image backup is complete, Windows asks if you want to create a system repair disc. You don't need a system repair disc if you have a USB recovery drive (described later in this chapter), so click No. If you don't have a USB recovery drive and you don't have a USB flash drive to create one, click Yes, instead.

Using the Windows Recovery Environment

You can perform many troubleshooting tasks from within Windows. For example, you can shut down and restart a program, uninstall a program or device, update a device driver, restore a previous version of a file from your history, and so on. Even signing off and then signing in or rebooting your computer will often solve many problems.

However, there are more intractable problems that require you to leave Windows and enter what is known as the *Recovery Environment* (or RE). The RE offers a simple, easily navigated set of screens that gives you access to a number of troubleshooting and recovery-related tools and utilities.

Understanding the Recovery Environment's tools

The Windows RE includes a number of tools that can help you get your system back on its feet. These tools include the following:

- **Startup Repair.** Analyzes your system startup and then attempts several repair strategies, which is useful if you're having problems starting Windows.

- **Uninstall Updates.** Enables you to remove a recent Windows update, which is useful if a problem began after installing that update.

● **Startup Settings.** Displays a set of commands that enable you to customize the way Windows starts:

  • **Enable Debugging.** Enables remote debugging of the Windows kernel.

  • **Enable Boot Logging.** Logs the boot process in a text file named ntbtlog.txt.

  • **Enable Low-Resolution Video.** Loads with the display set to 640x480 and 256 colors.

  • **Enable Safe Mode.** Enables you to run a barebones version of Windows (this is called *Safe Mode*) for troubleshooting.

  • **Enable Safe Mode with Networking.** Starts Windows in Safe Mode and also enables network support.

  • **Enable Safe Mode with Command Prompt.** Starts Windows in Safe Mode and also enables support for the Command Prompt.

  • **Disable Driver Signature Enforcement.** Prevents Windows from checking whether device drivers have digital signatures.

  • **Disable Early Launch Anti-Malware Protection.** Prevents Windows from scanning device drivers for malware during startup.

  • **Disable Automatic Restart After Failure.** Prevents Windows from restarting automatically when the system crashes.

  • **Launch Recovery Environment.** Starts Windows and automatically displays the RE.

● **Command Prompt.** Enables you to run command-line tools and utilities.

● **System Restore.** Enables you to revert to an earlier configuration (see later in this chapter).

● **System Image Recovery.** Enables you to restore your entire configuration from a system image backup (see earlier in this chapter).

Accessing the Recovery Environment

Here are the steps to follow to access and navigate the Recovery Environment:

1. **In the taskbar's Search box, type** recovery.

2. **Click Recovery options.** The Settings app runs and displays the Recovery tab.

3. **Under Advanced Startup, click Restart Now.** Window reboots your PC and displays the Choose an Option screen.

4. **Click Troubleshoot.** Windows displays the Troubleshoot screen. Note that on this screen you can click Reset Your PC to wipe your hard drive and reinstall Windows (see Chapter 10).

5. **Click Advanced Options.** Windows displays the Advanced Options screen. The screen you see will look similar to the one shown in Figure 12.4.

12.4 Use the Advanced Options screen to select a troubleshooting tool.

6. **Click a troubleshooting tool and follow the instructions that appear.** If you want to restart Windows for troubleshooting, click Startup Settings to display the Startup Settings screen.

7. **Click Restart.** Windows restarts your PC and then displays the Startup Settings screen, shown in Figure 12.5.

8. **Press the number of the command you want to run.** Windows starts using the mode specified by the command you chose. If you start your computer in Safe Mode, Windows displays "Safe Mode" in each corner of the screen, as shown in Figure 12.6.

12.5 Use the Startup Settings screen to restart Windows for troubleshooting.

12.6 Windows booted in Safe Mode.

If you can't start Windows, you can still access the advanced startup options as long as you have a USB recovery drive. If you have a USB recovery drive, boot to it, as I describe later in this chapter.

Working with a Recovery Drive

We all hope our computers operate trouble-free over their lifetimes, but we know from bitter experience that this is rarely the case. Computers are incredibly complex systems, so it is almost inevitable that a PC will develop glitches. If your hard drive is still accessible, you can boot to Windows and access the Recovery Environment, as described earlier in this chapter.

If you can't boot your PC, however, then you must boot using some other drive. If you have your Windows installation media, you can boot using that drive. If you don't have the installation media, you can still recover if you've created a USB recovery drive. This is a USB flash drive that contains the Windows Recovery Environment, which enables you to reset your PC, use System Restore, recover a system image, access startup options, and more.

Creating the recovery drive

Here are the steps to follow to format a USB flash drive as a Windows recovery drive:

1. **Connect a USB flash drive to your PC.** The drive should have a capacity of at least 16GB.

2. **In the taskbar's Search box, type** recovery.

3. **Click Recovery Drive.** The User Account Control dialog box appears.

4. **Type the password or PIN of your PC's administrator account.** The Recovery Drive Wizard appears.

5. **Click Next.** The Recovery Drive Wizard prompts you to choose the USB flash drive.

6. **Click the drive you inserted in Step 1, if it's not selected already (see Figure 12.7), and then click Next.** The Recovery Drive Wizard warns you that all the data on the drive will be deleted.

7. **Click Create.** The wizard formats the drive and copies the recovery tools and data.

8. **Click Finish.** You can now boot your PC using the recovery drive instead of your hard drive (as I describe in the next section).

×

← 🖴 Recovery Drive

Select the USB flash drive

The drive must be able to hold at least 16 GB, and everything on the drive will be deleted.

Available drive(s)
└ D:\ (FLASH DRIVE)

Next   Cancel

12.7 Select the USB flash drive you want to use as your PC's recovery drive.

Booting your PC using the recovery drive

To make sure your recovery drive works properly, you should test it by booting your PC to the drive. Here are the steps to follow:

1. **Insert the recovery drive.**

2. **Restart your PC.** How you boot to the drive depends on your system. Some PCs display a menu of boot devices, and you choose the USB drive from that menu. In other cases, you see a message telling you to press a key (such as F2) to access your PC's UEFI or BIOS settings; once you're in those settings, look for the option that sets the USB drive as the boot device.

3. **Click a keyboard layout.** The Choose an Option screen appears.

4. **If you want to reinstall Windows from the recovery drive, click Recover from a Drive.** Otherwise, you have two choices:

   - Click Troubleshoot to access the Recovery Environment's troubleshooting tools.

   - Click Continue to boot Windows normally.

Working with Restore Points

If your computer crashes or becomes unstable after you install a program or a new device, the System Restore feature in Windows can fix things by restoring the system to an earlier state. To ensure this works, you need to set restore points before you install programs and devices on your computer.

Creating a system restore point

Windows automatically creates system restore points as follows: every week (called a *system checkpoint*); before installing an update; and before installing certain programs (such as Microsoft Office) and devices. These are useful, but it pays to err on the side of caution and create your own restore points more often. This is particularly true if you're installing older programs or devices that might not work well with Windows or that aren't certified to be compatible with Windows. These programs and devices can create system instabilities, so having a restore point to fall back on ensures that you can return your system to a fully functioning state.

Follow these steps to create a system restore point:

1. **In the taskbar's Search box, type** restore.

2. **Click Create a Restore Point.** The User Account Control dialog box appears.

3. **Type the password or PIN of your PC's administrator account.** The System Properties dialog box appears.

4. **Click Create.** If the Create button is disabled, click Configure, click the Turn On System Protection radio button, and then click OK. The Create a Restore Point dialog box appears.

5. **Type a description for your restore point and then click Create.** System Restore creates the restore point.

6. **Click Close.**

7. **Click OK to close the System Properties dialog box.**

Reverting to an earlier restore point

If after you install a program or device you notice problems with your system, the easiest solution is to uninstall the item. If that doesn't work, then your next step is to revert to an earlier restore point. Windows reverts your computer to the configuration it had when you created the restore point, which should solve the problem.

Increasing Restore Point Storage

By default, Windows sets aside between three and five percent of your hard disk space for restore points. When that space is used up, Windows deletes the oldest restore points as new ones are added. If you use restore points frequently and you have a lot of free space on your hard drive, consider increasing the amount of space allotted to restore points. Follow Steps 1 to 4 to open the System Properties dialog box, click Configure, and then adjust the Max Usage slider to the percentage value you want to use.

Note, too, that reverting to an earlier restore point is a useful way to solve a malware problem. If you accidentally allow a virus, Trojan horse, or spyware onto your PC, it's almost impossible to get rid of these programs manually. Anti-malware software is usually the best solution, but some malware blocks the use of these programs. You can almost always get rid of malware by booting to Safe Mode (see earlier in this chapter) and then reverting to a restore point that predates the infection.

Here are the steps to follow to revert your system to an earlier restore point:

1. **In the taskbar's Search box, type** restore.

2. **Click Create a Restore Point.** The User Account Control dialog box appears.

3. **Type the password or PIN of your PC's administrator account.** The System Properties dialog box appears.

4. **Click System Restore.** The System Restore dialog box appears.

5. **Click Next.** System Restore prompts you to choose a restore point.

6. **Click the restore point you want to apply.** If you don't see the restore point you want, click the Show More Restore Points check box, as shown in Figure 12.8.

7. **Click Next.** The Confirm Your Restore Point dialog box appears.

8. **Click Finish.** System Restore asks you to confirm that you want to restore your system.

9. **Click Yes.** System Restore applies the restore point and then restarts Windows.

System Restore ×

Restore your computer to the state it was in before the selected event

Current time zone: GMT-4:00

Date and Time	Description	Type
8/7/2020 2:34:23 PM	Installing old device	Manual
8/3/2020 12:42:20 PM	Automatic Restore Point	System
7/23/2020 4:57:26 PM	Automatic Restore Point	System
7/15/2020 1:33:21 PM	Windows Update	Windows Update

☑ Show more restore points   Scan for affected programs

< Back   Next >   Cancel

12.8 Choose the restore point you want to use.

Index

A

accounts
 adding contacts from existing, 60–62
 adding for email, 44–46
 changing names for email, 46–47
 customizing sync settings for email, 48
 deleting for email, 47
 managing for email, 44–47
 switching between email, 51
activity history, clearing, 201–202
activity reporting, enabling, 130
Administrator user account, 126
albums, viewing images by, 104–105
all-day events, creating in calendars, 73
apps. *See also specific apps*
 accessing settings for, 6–7
 adding to Lock screen, 17–18
 moving between desktops, 22
 pinning to Start menu, 7–8
 pinning to taskbar, 10–11
 quitting to save energy, 153
 removing to free up space, 224
 specifying when opening documents, 185–186
 stopping notifications for, 201
aspect ratio, 102, 108

B

background (Lock screen), 16–17
badges, showing on taskbar buttons, 12
battery options, 149–154
Bluetooth, 154, 196–197
bold, 162
booting PCs using recovery drives, 234
browsing history, deleting, 209–211
bulleted lists, creating in OneNote app, 173

C

cache, 209–211
Calendar app
 adding event reminders to calendar, 74
 adding events to calendar, 72–73
 creating recurring events, 73–74
 customizing calendar, 76–77
 setting up online meetings, 74–76
 viewing calendar, 71–72
Camera app, taking pictures/video with PC camera, 101–102
Camera Roll, 101
Change permission, for shared folders, 136–137
Character Map, 165–167
children, sharing PCs with, 127–132

clarity, adjusting in images in Photos app, 115

clearing activity history, 201–202

collection, viewing images by, 104–105

color, adjusting in images in Photos app, 114–115

Command Prompt tool, 230

Compact layout, for touch keyboard, 144

contacts
  adding from existing accounts, 60–62
  assigning photos to, 65–67
  combining, 70
  creating, 62–64, 67–68
  creating from electronic business cards, 67–68
  deleting, 70
  editing, 65
  filtering, 68–69
  hiding by accounts, 69
  hiding without phone numbers, 68
  linking multiple profiles to, 69–70
  locating, 70
  searching for, 64–65
  suggested, 69–70
  viewing, 64–65

content, restricting for user accounts, 131–132

cookies, 209–212

Cortana Voice Assistant, 83–85

cropping images in Photos app, 107–108

D

day, viewing events by, 72

Default layout, for touch keyboard, 144

Delete command, 181–182

desktop mode, hiding taskbar in, 11

desktops
  adding, 20–21
  extending with multiple monitors, 18–20
  setting picture as background for, 104

setting up multiple, 20–22

switching between, 21–22

using multiple, 81

digital cameras, importing images from, 98–99

directions. See Maps app

Disk Cleanup, 224

documents
  copying, 167
  creating, 158
  defined, 158
  editing, 158–167
  finding text in, 162–164
  inserting special symbols in, 165–167
  opening, 159–160
  replacing text in, 164–165
  saving, 158–159
  searching for, 160
  sharing, 132–134

Documents folder. See documents

Double-tap gesture, 142

Dynamic Lock, activating, 198

E

electronic business cards, creating contacts from, 67–68

email
  accounts for children, 128
  adding accounts, 44–46
  blocking images in, 216–217
  changing account names, 46–47
  changing message priority, 54
  combining Focused and Other tabs, 49
  controlling notifications, 50–51
  creating an address, 121
  creating signatures, 51–52
  customizing account sync settings, 48
  deleting accounts, 47
  deleting messages, 216

email *(continued)*
  grouping messages, 49–50
  incoming message options, 47–51
  managing accounts, 44–47
  preventing from opening automatically, 216
  running spell-checker, 55–56
  security for, 215–218
  send options, 51–56
  setting default message font, 52–54
  switching between accounts, 51
  viruses in, 215–216
events. *See* Calendar app
extracting files from compressed folders, 183–185

F

Family tab, 130
Favorites bar, 31–33
Favorites list, 30–31, 33
file and folder management. *See also* documents
  changing file view, 176
  changing folder system in Photos app, 99
  copying files, 178
  creating files, 180–181
  deleting files, 181–182, 225–226
  extracting files from compressed folders, 183–185
  inserting files in OneNote app, 172
  moving files, 178–179
  previewing files, 176–177
  protecting folders with advanced file permissions, 136–137
  renaming files, 179–180
  renaming folders, 136
  restoring deleted files, 182
  restoring files from history, 227–228
  saving file history, 226–227
  scanning downloaded files, 207
  searching from folder windows, 83

  selecting files, 175–176
  sharing folders, 132–134, 135–136
  specifying apps when opening documents, 185–186
File Explorer
  creating documents from, 158
  opening folders using, 160
  previewing files in, 177
  rotating images using, 111
  scanning downloaded file from, 207
  searching folders using, 83
  starting slide shows using, 106
  viewing images using, 103–104
file view, changing, 176
filters, applying to images, 108–109
Find feature, 162–164
fingerprint sign-ins, setting up, 194–195
first-party cookie, 211
flash drives, checking free space on, 224
Focused tab, combining with Other tab, 49
folders. *See* file and folder management
fonts
  changing for text in documents, 160–162
  customizing, 39–40
  guidelines for using, 162
  setting default email message, 52–54
formatting text notes in OneNote app, 171
Full Control permission, for shared folders, 136–137

G

gestures, 141–143, 148
Global Positioning System (GPS), 87, 212–214
Google contacts, adding, 60–62
groups, 49–50, 136–137

H

Handwriting panel, 145, 147–148
hard disk, checking free space for, 223–225
hiding taskbar, 11–12

I

iCloud contacts, adding, 61

images

adding to notebook pages in OneNote app, 172

adding vignette effects to, 110

applying filters to, 108–109

assigning to contacts, 65–67

blocking in email messages, 216–217

changing for user accounts, 125–126

cropping in Photos app, 107–108

importing from smartphones/digital cameras, 98–99

rotating in Photos app, 111

scanning, 99–101

straightening in Photos app, 111–112

taking with PC camera, 101–102

using Spot Fix tool on, 116

viewing, 103–107

IMAP accounts, adding, 45–46

importing images from smartphones/digital cameras, 98–99

InPrivate browsing feature, 211

interlaced scanning, 102

Internet security

blocking images in email messages, 216–217

choosing to not save passwords for websites, 208

deleting browsing history, 209–211

deleting saved website passwords, 208–209

enabling tracking prevention, 212–213

phishing scams, 217–218

preventing ad sites from tracking, 211–212

preventing email messages opening automatically, 216

preventing sites from requesting location, 213–215

turning on private browsing, 211

viruses, 206–207, 215–216

italic, 162

J

join gesture, 148

K

Keep My Files option, 203

keyboard shortcuts

for bold, 162

for copying files, 178

for cutting files, 179

for italic, 162

for opening documents, 160

for opening Preview pane, 177

for pasting files, 178, 179

for running Rename command, 180

for saving documents, 159

for selecting files, 176

for underline, 162

L

launch location (Weather app), 94–95

light, adjusting for images in Photos app, 112–113

linking multiple profiles to contacts, 69–70

links, opening in tabs, 26

locations. See Maps app; Weather app

Lock screen, 15–18

locking PCs, 195–198

M

Mail app, vCard format and, 67. See also email

maintenance

booting PCs using recovery drives, 234

checking hard disk free space, 223–225

creating recovery drives, 233–234

creating system image backups, 228–229

creating system restore points, 235

deleting unnecessary files, 225–226

favorites, 33

restoring files from history, 227–228

maintenance *(continued)*

   reverting to earlier restore points, 235–237

   saving file history, 226–227

   scheduling automatic, 222–223

   Windows Recovery Environment, 229–233

Map Views (Maps app), 93

Maps app, 87–93

Match Case check box, in searches, 164, 165

memory card, checking free space on, 224

Microsoft 365 contacts, adding, 60

Microsoft account, 120–121

Microsoft Edge, customizing, 34–40

monitors, extending desktop with multiple, 18–20

month, viewing events by, 71

N

navigating tabs, 28

network, sharing folders with others on, 135–136

notebooks. *See* OneNote app

notification area (taskbar), 13–15

notifications, 50–51, 201

numbered lists, creating in OneNote app, 173–174

O

OneNote app

   adding images to notebook pages in, 172

   adding pages/sections to notebooks in, 168–170

   adding text notes in, 170–172

   creating notebooks in, 168

   deleting notebooks in, 168

   tags, 175

   working with notebook lists in, 173–175

   working with text notes in, 170–172

online ads, 207

Only Allow These Websites check box, 132

Other tab, combining with Focused tab, 49

P

pages

   adding to Favorites list, 30–31

   adding to notebooks in OneNote app, 168–170

   opening from Favorites list, 33

Paint app, scanning images into, 101

pairing Bluetooth mobile devices, 196–197

passwords

   choosing to not save for websites, 208

   creating, 190–193

   deleting saved website, 208–209

   forgotten, 124–125

   picture, 192–193

   updating for accounts, 191

PCs. *See also* tablet PC

   booting using recovery drives, 234

   configuring to lock automatically, 196

   controlling with Cortana, 84–85

   locking, 195–198

   resetting, 202–203

   searching, 80–83

   sharing resources, 132–137

   sharing via user accounts, 120–127

   sharing with children, 127–132

   synchronizing settings between, 6

   taking pictures/video with camera on, 101–102

Peek feature, 12

People app

   adding contacts from existing accounts, 60–62

   assigning photos to contacts, 65–67

   creating contacts, 62–64

   creating contacts from electronic business cards, 67–68

   deleting contacts, 70

   editing contacts, 65

   filtering contacts, 68–69

including contacts on meeting invites from, 75

linking multiple profiles to contacts, 69–70

viewing contacts, 64–65

permissions. *See* sharing

phishing scams, 217–218

Photos app

adding vignette effects to images, 110

adjusting clarity in images, 115

adjusting color in images, 114–115

adjusting light for images, 112–113

applying filters to images, 108–109

cropping images, 107–108

enhancing images, 107–110

importing images from smartphones/ digital cameras, 98–99

removing red eye from images, 115–116

repairing images, 111–116

rotating images, 111

scanning images, 99–101

starting slide shows in, 106–107

straightening images, 111–112

using Spot Fix tool, 116

viewing images using, 104–105

Photos tile, running slide shows on, 106–107

Pictures folder, 99

Pinch gesture, 142

pinning, 7–8, 10–11, 28

PINs, signing in with, 193–194

POP accounts, adding, 45–46

pop-up windows, 207

Power icon, 150, 152

power options, 149–154

Preview pane, 176–177

priority, changing for email messages, 54

privacy, 84, 85. *See also* security

private browsing, turning on, 211

profiles, linking to contacts, 69–70

progressive scanning, 102

Q

quality, of images/videos, 102

quitting apps to save energy, 153

R

Read permission, for shared folders, 136, 137

recovery drives, 233–234

Recycle Bin, 182

red eye, removing from images in Photos app, 115–116

Remove Everything option, 203

Replace feature, 164–165

resetting computers, 202–203

restrictions, 128–132

S

Save As command, 167

saving

copies of documents, 167

documents, 158–159

favorite pages, 30–33

file history, 226–227

scanning, 99–101, 207

screen brightness, adjusting, 151

screen time, setting limits for, 130–131

Search box (taskbar), 6

Search feature, 64–65, 80–83, 160

sections, adding to notebooks in OneNote app, 168–170

security. *See also* Internet security

clearing activity history, 201–202

controlling private information, 199–200

creating passwords, 190–191

creating picture passwords, 192–193

locking PC, 195–198

resetting computer, 202–203

setting up fingerprint sign-ins, 194–195

signing in with PINs, 193–194

security *(continued)*
  Start menu, 198–199
  stopping app notifications, 201
  updating account passwords, 191
  ZIP files, 183
setting(s)
  accessing for apps, 6–7
  battery options, 149–154
  default email message font, 52–54
  default zoom level, 36–37
  opening Settings app, 4–6
  pictures as desktop background, 104
  power mode, 150–151
  power options, 149–154
  restrictions on child user accounts,
    128–132
  screen time limits, 130–131
  Start menu, 9–10
  synchronizing between PCs, 6
  taskbar, 11–13
Settings app, 4–6, 82, 147
setup
  fingerprint sign-ins, 194–195
  multiple desktops, 20–22
  online meetings on calendars, 74–76
sharing
  documents, 132–134
  folders, 132–134
  folders with others on network, 135–136
  PC resources, 132–137
  PC via user accounts, 120–127
  PCS with children, 127–132
  switching to advanced, 134
Sharing Wizard, 132–134, 135
signatures, email, 51–52
signing in, with PINs, 193–194
Skype app, 85–87
sleep mode, 154
Slide gesture, 142
slide shows, starting in Photos app, 106–107

smartphones, importing images from, 98–99
special effects, 161
special symbols, inserting in documents,
  165–167
spell-checker, running in emails, 55–56
Split layout, for touch keyboard, 144
Spot Fix tool (Photos app), 116
Spread gesture, 142
Standard layout, for touch keyboard,
  144–145
Standard user account, 126
Start menu, 7–10, 198–199
Startup Repair tool, 229
Startup Settings tool, 230
startup tabs, 28–30, 123–124
stylus, 141
subfolders, 159, 167, 181
Swipe gesture, 142
system image backups, creating, 228–229
System Image Recovery tool, 230
System Restore, 230, 235–237

T

tablet mode, 12, 140–141
tablet PC
  about, 139
  adjusting screen brightness, 151
  configuring touch keyboard, 149
  controlling Windows with gestures,
    141–143
  creating custom power plans, 152–153
  displaying touch keyboard, 143–144
  entering text using handwriting panel,
    147–148
  inputting text with touch keyboard,
    143–149
  monitoring battery life, 150
  selecting touch keyboard type, 144–145
  setting power and battery options,
    149–154
  setting power mode, 150–151

sleep mode, 154
switching to Battery Saver mode, 151–152
Tablet mode, 140–141
using touch keyboard, 145–146
tabs
closing, 30
creating, 26
customizing, 26–28
duplicating, 28
navigating, 28
opening links in, 26
pinning, 28
reopening closed, 30
tags (OneNote app), 175
Talk to Cortana icon, 84
Tap and hold gesture, 142
Tap gesture, 142
Task View feature, 80, 81
taskbar
customizing, 10–15
notification area, 13–15
pinning apps to, 10–11
Search box, 6
searching from, 82
settings, 11–13
tasks, minimizing to save energy, 154
text
changing font of in documents, 160–162
entering using Handwriting panel, 147–148
finding in documents, 162–164
inputting with touch keyboard, 143–149
replacing in documents, 164–165
text notes, adding in OneNote app, 170–172
themes, changing, 35–36
third-party content, controlling, 61–62
third-party cookie, 211–212
time-based events, creating in calendars, 72–73

timeline, viewing, 80
Tint slider (Photos app), 114
titles, adding to images in OneNote app, 172
to-do lists, creating in OneNote app, 174
toolbar, customizing, 37–38
touch keyboard, 143–149
Touch Keyboard icon, 144
touch PC. See tablet PC
traffic information, viewing on Maps app, 93
Turn gesture, 142
2-in-1 devices, 139
type size, 161
type style, 161
typefaces. See font

U
underline, 162
Uninstall Updates tool, 229
user accounts
changing pictures for, 125–126
changing type of, 126–127
creating, 120–122
deleting, 127
restricting content for, 131–132
setting restrictions on child, 128–132
sharing PCs via, 120–127
switching between, 122–125

V
vCard format, 67–68
vignette effects, adding to images, 110
viruses, 206–207, 215–216
voice commands, in Cortana Voice Assistant, 83–85

W
wake word, 85
Warmth slider (Photos app), 114
Weather app, 93–95

web browsing
adding pages to Favorites list, 30–31
changing Edge search engine, 34–35
changing themes, 35–36
closing tabs, 30
controlling startup tabs, 28–30
creating tabs, 26
customizing font, 39–40
customizing tabs, 26–28
customizing toolbar, 37–38
duplicating tabs, 28
Favorites bar, 31–33
maintaining favorites, 33
navigating tabs, 28
opening links in tabs, 26
opening pages from Favorites list, 33
pinning tabs, 28
setting default zoom level, 36–37

web security. See Internet security
web-based email accounts, adding, 44–45
Webdings typeface, 167
websites. See Internet security
week, viewing events by, 71–72
widening Start menu, 9
Wi-Fi, turning off to save energy, 154
Windows (Microsoft), 141–143
windows, searching from folder, 83
Windows Recovery Environment, 229–233
Wingdings typeface, 167

Z

ZIP files, 183–184
Zoom In/Out icon (Maps app), 89
zoom level, setting default, 36–37